FIRST THE KINGDOM

A Call to the Conservative Pentecostal/
Charismatics and the Liberal Social Justice
Advocates for Repentance and Reunification

Stephen A. Graham
The University of Indianapolis
Marcia W. Graham

UNIVERSITY
PRESS OF
AMERICA

Lanham • New York • London

University Press of America®, Inc.
4720 Boston Way
Lanham, Maryland 20706

3 Henrietta Street
London WC2E 8LU England

Printed in the United States of America
British Cataloging in Publication Information Available

Library of Congress Cataloging-in-Publication Data

Graham, Stephen A.
First the kingdom : a call to the conservative Pentecostal/charismatics and the liberal social justice advocates for repentance and reunification / Stephen A. Graham, Marcia W. Graham.
p. cm.
Includes bibliographical references and index.
1. Christian union—United States. 2. Pentecostalism and Christian union. 3. Liberalism (Religion)—Protestant churches. 4. Church—Unity. 5. Reconciliation—Religious aspects—Protestant churches. I. Graham, Marcia W. II. Title.
BX9.5.P45G73 1994 270.82—dc20 93–36075 CIP

ISBN 0–8191–9327–5 (cloth : alk. paper)
ISBN 0–8191–9328–3 (pbk. : alk. paper)

™ The paper used in this publication meets the minimum requirements of American National Standard for Information Sciences—Permanence of Paper for Printed Library Materials, ANSI Z39.48–1984.

DEDICATION

With hearts' praise and gratitude to God we dedicate this book to my parents, Vera and Thomas Graham, whose generosity enabled us to do the necessary research and to our Prayer and Praise Fellowship at Chapel Hill United Methodist Church whose prayers have been indispensable.

"A man can receive nothing, except it be given him from heaven."

John 3:27KJV

Contents

Preface: Why We Wrote This Book

STEPHEN: This book is our hymn of praise to God and to the power of His Holy Spirit in the Body of Jesus Christ, the Church, in the United States today. As mainline Protestants who were baptized, nurtured and trained in the Southern Baptist, United Methodist, Episcopalian and Presbyterian churches and in their colleges and universities, we confess our facile assumption that the liberal theology we learned and lived was both the necessary and sufficient condition of our Christian discipleship.

We are charismatic and support many charismatic ministries. We also support those concerns which most closely approximate Kingdom justice. We do so because we are grateful for social and political action and economic justice which are as much evidences of the grace and presence of God as saving souls, healing the sick and speaking in tongues are evidences of the gifts and power of the Holy Spirit.

MARCIA: In 1977 God met me at the point of my need, following the death of my father, in the person of Oral Roberts. In 1982, as part of my spiritual formation, I bacame more politicized. As collegians in the 1960s both my husband and I were mildly -- not completely radically -- politicized. That tumultuous era did not permit ease. Moral passions, dilemmas, and political tensions went with the territory. Senseless escalation in the mud of Southeast Asia became an unconscionable conflict called Vietnam. That, together with a political and legal revolution called Civil Rights and a social shake-up called the Feminist Movement, colored everybody's private little world, if they were at all ethically sensitized. So I demonstrated, vigiled, fasted and engaged in relatively safe forms of dissent and protestation. In between assassinations during the turbulent '60s, we mostly agonized and tried to get on with living the proverbial American dream gone somehow acidly haywire.

In 1982 the omnipresent, direst political and social justice issues ever invented -- nuclear annihilation, global pollution, torture, human rights deprivation and violation, terrorism, rampant economic exploitation, apartheid, racism, low-intensity proxy warfare in Central America, genocide(Uganda and Cambodia), hunger, famine, to name a few -- and their accompanying worthwhile causes/appeals streamed into my consciousness with screaming harpy-like fury. Bulging manila files attest to heavy correspondence with Congressmen and elected officials. More peaceful vigils ensued.

In 1985 I discovered John Wesley and E. Stanley Jones. In 1987 I received the infilling of the Holy Spirit and released my prayer language. Then came 1988 and "Word Explosion" at Victory Christian Center in Tulsa, Oklahoma.

Never discount bathrooms as potential holy ground. In 1988, while standing in the bathroom of the Grand View Hotel, looking in the mirror, these words came: "I want you to help call My Church to repentance." They were not repeated. As you might expect I wondered greatly. For three years I have questioned, questioned, questioned. In between questioning -- 'Did I really hear that?' 'Why *me*?' 'What does this mean, really?' 'How?' -- I doubted. I prayed for clarification, confirmation. Not until the completion of this book, have I told anyone except Stephen about what I 'heard' in that Tulsa bathroom. Despite authentic assurances that we were "on the right track" with this Divinely commisssioned book, as it were, I still doubted. Not until the completion of this book did God give me *the* confirming word I really needed. Would you believe that it came to me in our bathroom while I was reading *My Utmost for His Highest*? No sudden shock, no ninety-nine spine-tingling goose bumps, no racing heart beat. Just a knowing that I knew that I knew. The words I read were these:

> I know when the proposition comes from God because of its quiet persistence: When I have to weigh the *pros* and *cons*, and doubt and debate come in, I am bringing in an element that is not of God, and I come to the conclusion that the suggestion was not a right one. .... Loyalty to Jesus means I have to step out where I do not see anything (cf. Matt. xiv. 29); loyalty to my notions means that I clear the ground first by my intelligence. Faith is not intelligent understanding, faith is deliberate commitment to a Person where I see no way. .... Obey

> Him with glad reckless joy. When He says something and you begin to debate, it is because you have a conception of His honour which is not His honour. Are you loyal to Jesus or loyal to your notion of Him? Are you loyal to what He says, or are you trying to compromise with conceptions which never came from Him? "Whatsoever He saith unto you, *do it.*"[1]

You see, the words that I heard have persisted with a "quiet persistence." Did I obey with "glad reckless joy"? No, I'm pretty sure I haven't exhibited that kind of obedience. But I did do what I knew to do.

Do Stephen or I understand fully why our spiritual pilgrimage has taken the turns and twists it has? Not even remotely. We only "see in part." Do we presume to know why the ever-surprising God in His improbable ways picked us two improbable unlikelies to write a book that would say, "Hey, Church, stop grieving the Holy Spirit. Enough of this disgraceful dichotomy between conservative pentecostal-charismatics (who we are) and liberal social justice advocates (who we are). Repent. Quit being suspicious, sniping and separate."? Do I know why I clipped a page from *The Upper Room* dated June 24, 1986, put an asterisk by these lines: **"The Bible records that God has sometimes sprung real surprises. Never could the people have anticipated some of God's moves."**[2] (Emphasis added.) and added a postscript which I copied from an earlier meditation, which reads: **"God's messages are often hidden in daily events and people and circumstances."?**[3] The answer is that I don't know why except we have been two of those people who could never have anticipated God's move in our lives in just this way and that we fit that category of "daily people" in whom God has chosen to hide his message. I am prompted to quote these out-of-context words of John the Baptist: "For he whom God hath sent speaketh the words of God: for God giveth not the Spirit by measure unto him." (John 3:34KJV).

And, again, I do not know why except that this message from *The Upper Room* seems to fit into this little picture puzzle called "Why We Wrote This Book." It also fits into the bigger picture puzzle called "How the Holy Spirit has integrated and is integrating our seemingly disparate experiences of God, our personal witness and involvement, together with our frustration, questions, limitations and failures, and even our affiliation with the United Methodist Church which has a special position (theologically and actually) in the Body -- because of its history of strong experiential faith and social justice consciousness and commitment -- to spearhead a recapturing and reemulating of the revolutionizing and radicalizing Kingdom of God pattern initiated at Pentecost." (See the Book of Acts).

This book has come about, we believe, because God's Holy Spirit has become "mighty tired" of this split in His Church between conservative pentecostal-charismatics and liberal social justice adherents. Stanley Jones says, "When God gets mighty tired of a wrong, He uses any instrument He can get hold of if His own people won't respond."[4] For the reason that we are willing to be that "instrument," God is willing to use this book to call the Church to repent. However, our motives are not unmixed. We're getting tired too. Tired of the schizophrenia that tries to attach itself to us (and to others?) to inhibit us from giving full expression to our experiences of God and to Kingdom truth as we perceive it on those occasions when we're in either the pentecostal-charismatic fold or the social justice fold.

Stanley Jones also writes:

> Jesus offered the Kingdom of God to His own people -- they would be the agent of the coming of the new Order. They were bound by prejudice and ritual and wouldn't respond, so God grew tired and raised up the Church out of the nobodies. His own people were left standing behind a Wailing Wall.[5]

We cannot help but wonder whether the Church, if it persists in this sin of divison, will be "left standing behind a Wailing Wall" or worse.

Jesus told his disciples that He had many things to say to them but that they were not ready or able "to bear them now." If Jesus, who is the "unfolding Word,"[6] has anything to say to the Church through this book, we pray for grace for all to be ready and able to receive Jesus' "more."

We conclude this statement of purpose and explanatory word with the words of the person who is teaching us well to be first receptive, then active and responsive. Stanley Jones says,

> If Christ dwells in your heart, you are the narrowest person in the world -- you are a man of one Person, one Allegiance, one Love -- you are One-centric. And yet you are universalized. You 'grasp' every dimension of life. You 'grasp' the truth in 'the Breadth' -- the liberals. You are more liberal than the liberals, for truth found anywhere belongs to you because you belong to the Truth, Christ. You 'grasp'

> the truth in 'the Length' -- the successionists, those who feel a sense of solidarity of the Christian centuries. You are more successionist than the Apostolic Successionists, for you are a Christ successionist -- all the Christians of the ages, not only the apostles, belong to you because you belong to Christ. You can 'grasp' the truth in 'the Depth' -- the fundamentalists, those who insist upon the Incarnation, the Atoning Death, the Resurrection. But you are more fundamental than the fundamentalists, for you are 'fixed and grounded' in the incarnate, atoning, resurrected Christ. He, and not merely doctrines about Him, is the fundamental center of your faith. And you can 'grasp' the truth of 'the Height' -- the mystics. But you are more mystic than the mystics, for you know 'the love of Christ which surpasses all knowledge.' -- the universal.[7]

We dare not give even the hint of an impression that this book comes with any air of finality. What we have written -- we firmly believe under the guidance of the Holy Spirit -- is not sacrosanct and uncorrectable. Its purpose will be accomplished if it enlarges our view of Christ the King and His Kingdom, helps us to 'grasp' the truth embodied in both wings -- conservative pentecostal-charismatic and liberal social justice -- of the Church, and tenderizes our hearts, individually and corporately, the one wing for the other. This book, from start to finish, is all of grace. Thank God that is so.

Chapters 1 - 5 and the Glossary were written by Stephen and the remaining three chapters 6 - 8 were written by Marcia.

Chapter 1, The Past, Present and Future of the Charismatic Renewal Movement, explores the origin and development of charismatic renewal in the United States. This chapter explains why the nineteenth century American evangelical movement lost its zeal for social, economic and political reform and separated into two different streams -- a conservative stream which stressed personal salvation and a liberal stream which emphasized social justice. Chapter 1 also describes the current status of the American charismatic renewal movement and suggests that in order to fulfill God's intention for His church charismatic renewal must bring its prophetic insight to bear on the whole gospel, including the gospel of social, economic and political salvation.

Chapter 2 evaluates both the strengths and the weaknesses of the charismatic renewal movement. This chapter also considers the growing social and political witness of the charismatic renewal movement and concludes with a discussion of the ecumenical nature of charismatic renewal.

Chapter 3, Weaknesses of Liberals and Conservatives, examines the contemporary consequences of the division between liberal and conservative Christians outlined in Chapter 1. Chapter 3 evaluates the argument that religious liberalism in the United States may be obsolete because of its endorsement of pluralism and relativism and because of its association with political extremism. Moreover, Chapter 3 points out the hypocrisy of religious conservatives who apply the gospel to individuals but not to institutions. The chapter concludes with a call for both liberals and conservatives to overcome their respective shortcomings and to proclaim the whole gospel of both personal and corporate salvation.

In Chapter 4 we state that the only way to bring conservative American charismatics and pentecostals together with the advocates of liberal social justice is through repentance. True Christian repentance which follows the biblical pattern of turning from sin must be both individual and corporate repentance in order to produce the spiritual fruit of renewal and restoration. Chapter 4 ends with three parables of repentance based on our experience at Indianapolis 1990, the Congress on the Holy Spirit and World Evangelization.

Chapter 5, One in Mind and Spirit, offers a wholistic statement of personal and corporate salvation based on the radical character of the New Testament church. Using John H. Yoder's biblical concept of revolutionary subordination, we offer an ethic of both personal and institutional conduct which embraces all of man's life in the kingdom of God.

Chapters 6, 7 and 8 use E. Stanley Jones' concept of the Kingdom of God as the hermeneutic and dynamic for reconciling the two divergent streams of American Christianity. Chapter 6 explains both the importance of the kingdom of God and the nature of the kingdom of God in the New Testament. Because Jesus always describes the kingdom of God in both personal and social terms in the New Testament gospels, the kingdom of God is the Holy Spirit's gift to the American church to reconcile liberal social justice advocates with conservative pentecostal/charismatics.

Chapter 7, The Disgraceful Disunity of the Church, continues our use of E. Stanley Jones' interpretation of the kingdom of God to explore the origin of the rift between conservative charismatics and pentecostals and liberal advocates of social justice in the United States.

The source of the split is identified in Acts 6:1-7, which records the first spearation of the material from the spiritual in the first century church when the 12 apostles instructed the church to appoint seven believers to distribute funds to the widows so that the apostles would be free to preach. Chapter 8 points to the kingdom of God as both the way out of this compartmentalization of the material from the spiritual as well as the way to unite liberal and conservatie American Christians.

Notes

1. Chambers, p. 88.
2. Bruce, p. 60.
3. Harden, p. 11.
4. Jones, 1946, p. 353.
5. *Ibid.*
6. Jones, 1931, p. 35.
7. Jones, 1946, p. 175.

ACKNOWLEDGMENTS

We cannot fully acknowledge all those who have contributed directly or indirectly to this book. However, we have noted in each chapter those sources (with full citation in the bibliography) whose ideas or words we have used. And at the end of chapters 1 - 6 we have included a section entitled, **For Further Reading and Reflection** which discusses and evaluates many books and articles in addition to those cited in the text of these chapters.

Moreover, we gratefully acknowledge those individuals and institutions who provided special information, advice and encouragement in our research. The University of Indianapolis granted Stephen sabbatical leave during Semester II of the 1990-91 academic year to work on this book. In the early stages of our research the staff of the excellent library at Asbury Theological Seminary were especially helpful. Paul G. Chappell, the Dean of the School of Theology and Mission at Oral Robers University was most generous in sharing his time and the use of the resources of his school with us. Others at ORU who helped us include Professor Henry I. Lederle; Dr. Khoo, the Theology Librarian; and James Zeigler, the Assistant Director and Librarian of the Holy Spirit Research Center. Dr. James B. Buskirk, Pastor and Senior Minister of the First United Methodist Church in Tulsa, gave us his anointed counsel and advice on reconciling conservative pentecostal and charismatic Christians with liberal social justice Christians.

Those who responded to our letters with valuable suggestions and additional sources were Leroy C. Hodapp, the Resident Bishop for the Indiana Area of the United Methodist Church; Mr. Bruce Robbins, the General Secretary of the General Commission on Christian Unity and Interreligious Concerns of the United Methodist Church; the Reverend Billy Joe Daugherty, Pastor of Victory Christian Center in Tulsa; the Honorable Paul B. Henry, Member of the U. S. House of Representatives; and Dr. Vinson Synan, Chairman of the North American Renewal Service Committee and Director of the Holy Spirit Research Center at ORU. Finally, we wish to thank Ms. Christine Guyonneau, the Reference Librarian at the University of Indianapolis, for her able assistance in obtaining materials through interlibrary loan; and Brad Bishop of the University of Indianapolis Computing Services for his indulgence and endless patience with our interminable questions about how Clarisworks works.

We are deeply indebted to Abingdon Press and very appreciative of Abingdon's Subsidiary Rights & Permissions Supervisor Ms. Bernadine Shaw for her splendid and gracious oversight in seeking permission to use excerpted material from several titles of E. Stanley Jones and Eunice Jones and James K. Mathews. We gratefully make the following acknowledgments:

From *The Way* by E. Stanley Jones. Copyright 1946 by Stone & Pierce. Copyright renewal 1974 by Mable Lossing Jones. Used by permission of the publisher, Abingdon Press.

From *The Christ of the Mount*, copyright renewal 1958 by E. Stanley Jones. Used by permission of the publisher, Abingdon Press.

From *The Unshakable Kingdom and the Unchanging Person*, E. Stanley Jones. Copyright 1972 by Abingdon Press. Used by permission.

From *Is the Kingdom of God Realism?* copyright renewal 1968 by E. Stanley Jones. Used by permission of the publisher, Abingdon Press.

From *The Choice Before Us,* copyright renewal 1965 by E. Stanley Jones. Used by permission of the publisher, Abingdon Press.

From *Selections from E. Stanley Jones: Christ and Human Need,* compiled by Eunice Jones Mathews and James K. Mathews. Copyright 1972 by Abingdon Press. Used by permission.

Chapter 1

The Past, Present and Future of the Charismatic Renewal Movement

In the 1950s Timothy Smith astounded the religious and academic world with his prize-winning research and writing on the intimate connection between religious revivals and social reform in nineteenth century America. Before Smith's work was published, historians interpreted religious fervor in the 1800s as a short-lived phenomenon of limited impact on the American western frontier. Smith's exhaustive research, however, demonstrated that religious revival was an integral part of American life and culture throughout the nineteenth century not only on the frontier but also in the cities of the Northeast and Midwest. Moreover, Smith demonstrated that Protestant evangelism was not confined to the pulpit and the pew but was the primary impetus for the abolition movement, for the struggle for women's rights and for the temperance crusade.

It is difficult for Americans today, who live in an almost completely secular culture, to fully appreciate the pervasive influence of Christianity throughout the nineteenth century. As early as the 1830s foreign visitors to the United States noted the broad scope of the impact of religion on American society. Alexis de Tocqueville, a French nobleman who visited America in the late 1820s, wrote that although there was no officially established church in the United States, American clergymen had an indirect but very powerful influence on the political and social life of the nation through public opinion, "mores" and the regulation of "domestic life."[1] So when Smith proposed his controversial thesis 120 years after Tocqueville left the United States and returned to France, he was merely rediscovering a long neglected truth. And since the appearance of Smith's book in 1957 other social scientists specializing in nineteenth century American studies have concluded that religion was *the* most important factor shaping the structure and function of political, economic and social institutions in the United States during the 1800s.[2]

Smith's book, *Revivalism and Social Reform in Mid-Nineteenth Century America*, is important and controversial not only because it described the full impact of Protestant evangelism in the United States during the nineteenth century, but also because it showed how American evangelists "helped prepare the way both in theory and in practice for what later became known as the social gospel."[3] Thus it was not liberal Protestant theology but conserative evangelical Christianity which expanded the role of the churches from the personal salvation of individual souls to the corporate redemption of public and private institutions.

This conclusion is still controversial. Donald W. Dayton, an authority on evangelicalism and pentecostal theology, concludes that "Just as the social gospel was a manifestation of a social conscience among theological liberals, there was also a disaffection with bourgeois church life among the more theologically conservative."[4] Dayton believes that the social gospel was the product of liberalism but that evangelical social reform was the result of dissatisfaction among conservative Protestants with the religious complacency of middle-class church life. The evangelical social movement was both more conservative and, in its critique of bourgeois life, more radical than the social gospel. Whose interpretation of the origin of the social gospel in late nineteenth and early twentieth century America -- Smith's or Dayton's -- is correct? The answer to this question is beyond the scope of this book. For our purposes the important point is that evangelicalism in the United States today is rooted in a nineteenth century tradition of evangelical social action.

The Evangelical Roots of Charismatic Renewal

The broad and deep involvement of nineteenth century evangelicalism in social, economic and political reform is important because the charismatic renewal movement, which has clearly revealed God's heart for revival among individual members of the body of Christ, is now facing the question of its prophetic witness to systemic and institutional injustice. As part of the twentieth century contemporary evangelical movement, will the charismatic renewal successfully integrate its powerful message of personal spiritual transformation with an equally powerful gospel of social, economic and political salvation?

In order to answer this question, we will look first at exactly how the wholistic doctrine of nineteenth century evangelicalism separated into conservative (personal redemption) and liberal (social justice) streams. Then we will describe the current status of the charismatic renewal movement. Finally, we will examine the problems and prospects for the future of charismatic renewal in American Protestant Christianity.

David Moberg, an evangelical Christian and a sociologist, identifies what he calls "the great reversal" or the shift of evangelicals from their traditional concern with social, political and economic issues to their contemporary preoccupation with personal redemption in the fundamentalist/modernist schism of the early 1900s.[5] Fundamentalists were especially concerned about the popularity of using the newly devised "scientific" criticism in Protestant seminaries. Modernism was the product of nineteenth century liberal theology and of the social gospel. Modernists eagerly sought to accomodate the Christian faith to the rapidly changing world of twentieth century America. Evangelicals, according to Moberg and according to most historians and sociologists of the evangelical movement, sided with the fundamentalists and against the modernists. The fundamentalist reaction against modernism, however, did not diminish evangelicals' concern for social ministry, which they continued to provide in the form of a wide variety of charitable programs. "The main difference was one of ideology and official polity: and of evangelical reluctance to address injustice in public and private *institutions*."[6]

Other theologians and commentators have traced the separation of evangelicalism into personal versus social redemption all the way back to the Protestant Reformation. Richard Lovelace, an evangelical theologian, says that classical evangelicalism has experienced the "Delta Effect," by which he means that the two broad streams of evangelicalism -- one emphasizing renewal, nurture and missions; the other stressing ecumenism and social reform -- have themselves separated into many smaller streams.[7]

Another popular group of explanations for the evangelical movement's loss of its nineteenth century social action ministry is sociological models of how religious movements evolve and change over time. Ernst Troeltsch, a German sociologist, described how a religious sect is born with little or no formal organization amidst the fervor of new converts and in opposition to the religious establishment of the day. As the sect attracts more and more members, it becomes more highly organized and acquires the formal structure of a bureaucracy in order to maintain itself and its members. The growth of the sect in size and in social and religious status changes its relationship to the established churches. Hostility between the sect and the religious establishment decreases and eventually the sect itself becomes a church, a full-fledged member of the religious establishment.[8] There are scores of examples of this process of a sect becoming a church in the history of Christianity. In this chapter, however, we will apply Troeltsch's model specifically to the American evangelical, pentecostal and charismatic movements.

Does Troeltsch's model help to explain American evangelicalism's loss of social emphasis in the twentieth century? Have evangelicals in the United States, who began as a sect in the early 1800s, become a church? In his book, *Discovering An Evangelical Heritage*, which the author describes as the product of his "struggle to reconcile the seemingly irreconcilable in his own experience: the Evangelical heritage in which he was reared and values bequeathed him by the student movement of the 1960s," Donald Dayton says yes, evangelicalism's evolution from a sect to a church does help explain its loss of emphasis on social action.[9]

The most ambitious recent attempt to apply sociological concepts to American evangelicalism, however, is James Davison Hunter's *Evalgelicalism: The Coming Generation.* Based on a survey of hundreds of students at nine evangelical liberal arts colleges and seven evangelical seminaries in the mid-1980s, Hunter concludes that evangelicalism in the United States, like liberal Protestantism, is adapting to the "modern world view" and that secular interests may become more important to American evangelicals than spiritual interests.[10]

The best explanation of American evangelicalism's emphasis on personal over social salvation in the twentieth century lies in that "peculiar institution" of the nineteenth century, the institution which Thomas Jefferson accurately predicted would precipitate a nation-rending crisis "like a firebell in the night" -- slavery. As Southerners who grew up under the abhorrent institutional evil of racial segregation enforced by the mandate of laws enacted by "democratically " elected representatives and who personally experienced the tumultuous civil rights revolution of the 1960s, we know it is impossible to underestimate the total impact of racism on the soul of America. This issue can only be accurately described in Biblical terms.

> Slavery, and the poison of racial prejudice which it created, was to be the nation's rock of offense. Its woe was not to be restricted to those from whom the offense came. The fathers had sinned, and the children's teeth were set on edge.[11]

Richard Lovelace writes that the doctrine that the gospel should be restricted to spiritual concerns and should not interfere with political, economic or social affairs "emerged before the Civil War as a conservative evangelical defense of resistance toward or postponement of abolition."[12] Although published 35 years ago in a book about mid-nineteenth century America, Timothy Smith's analysis of the questions raised by slavery among Protestant churches reads like a contemporary debate within the United Methodist General Conference (or any mainline Protestant or Catholic denominational assembly between liberals and conservatives) over whether Christians should focus on personal evangelism or on institutional sins like sexism and the nuclear arms race. Smith writes that among the questions raised by slavery for American Protestant Christians in the mid-nineteenth century were

> [w]hether the proper role of the churches in a democratic society was to regulate individual conduct or to impose Christian principles upon social and legal institutions. ... [a]nd ... whether Christians might do violence for loving ends.[13]

In this way the pre-Civil War evangelical revival split between conservatives who openly supported slavery, often by a literal interpretation of references to slavery in the Old and New Testaments, or who wanted to postpone its abolition until blacks were "ready" for freedom; and liberals who demanded the immediate abolition of slavery. During the 1840s and 1850s when most of the mainline Protestant denominations divided into separate Northern and Southern branches, the Northern denominations anguished over the moral and spiritual dilemma of how to keep their churches in the border states of Maryland, Kentucy and Missouri from defecting to the newly-formed Southern denominations. After the Methodists split into the Methodist Episcopal Church and the Methodist Episcopal Church South in 1844, the ME Church remained silent on the issue of slavery because the Northern bishops wanted to keep the border conference churches within the Northern church.[14]

Like many churches in these climatic years leading up to the Civil War, Methodists also faced the problem of whether to exclude slaveowners from membership. The Southern and border state argument against exclusion was that to deny slaveowners church membership would remove from fellowship those most in need of the gospel. The problem with this Southern and border state argument, of course, is that "moral conviction in the pulpit" yields to "the self-interest which was allowed to flourish in the pew. The ancient evangelical practice was to fence sinners out."[15] Again, this moral and spiritual dilemma over whether slaveowners could belong to the church, which agonized the consciences of sincere and well-intentioned Christians in the North, the border states and the South 150 years ago, has a very familiar, even contemporary ring. Are not landowners today who exploit migrant farmworkers financially and who force them to pick crops in fields freshly covered in carcinogenic pesticides "those most in need of the gospel?" Can the church justify excluding these landowners from its membership?

Another consequence of the Civil War schism between pro-slavery and anti-slavery evangelicals was the difference between the two groups' theology and interpretation of Scripture. Since both the Old and New Testaments refer to the institution of slavery without clearly condemning it as sinful, anti-slavery evangelicals interpreted the Bible as the most authoritative but not the final or exclusive revelation of God's will for man. The pro-slavery evangelicals, on the other hand, interpreted the Bible literally, which was consistent with their view that Scripture not only refers to but gives God's approval of slavery. As a result of this schism between evangelicals over slavery many in the Southern Bible Belt "have believed ever since that the good book was a shield against social innovation."[16]

The Pentecostal Roots of Charismatic Renewal

Having concluded our discussion of nineteenth century American evangelicalism we turn now to pentecostalism, which emerged in the late nineteenth and early twentieth century in the United States as an outgrowth of the evangelical movement and which in turn spawned the contemporary charismatic renewal.

Like evangelicalism pentecostalism began as a group of sects and has evolved into established churches. Also like the evangelical movement, pentecostals in the early years of their development made no real distinction between their personal witness on the one hand and their social and political witness on the other. For example, many pentecostals were pacifists both in the United States and abroad in the years before and during World War I. Responding to calls within the contemporary pentecostal community for more research on the early social and political involvement of pentecostals,[17] Jay Beaman's Master of Divinity Thesis at North American Baptist Seminary on pentecostal pacifism has been published as a book describing the origin, development and rejection of pacifist beliefs among pentecostals.

One of Beaman's sources is John Alexander Dowie of Edinburgh, Scotland, a pentecostal who pastored a Congregational church in a suburb of Sydney, Australia during the 1870s. Dowie's fervent inner spiritual commitment to the compassion and love of God were the source of his passion for justice, his hatred of racial discrimination, his appeal for pacifism, his belief in equal universal education and his zeal for divine healing.[18] Pentecostals today, however, are not noted for their involvement in social issues. There are many plausible explanations for this loss of pentecostal social and political involvement, just as there are many plausible explanations for the loss of nineteenth century American evangelicalism's involvement in social and political issues. One reviewer of Beaman's book suggests that "cultural accomodation" is the best explanation of the pentecostal rejection of pacifism.[19] Beaman himself states at the end of his Master's Thesis that pentecostals should ask themselves "whether they can long maintain their distinctive views about the church and the Holy Spirit, while becoming completely conformed to mainstream evangelical socio-religious views."[20]

The Growth of Charismatic Renewal

Both the pentecostal movement and the more recent charismatic renewal are "a response to the sickness of Western civilization." They provide "the transforming power of worship, and the daily looking for God's awesome, intervening presence."[21] The pentecostal and charismatic movements offer a personal experience with God and with other pentecostals and charismatics which liberal Protestant theology, with its almost exclusive emphasis on social justice, has not given to the body of Christ. In the 1960s American liberalism made what was perhaps its final and unsuccessful attempt to use institutional reform as a means of both personal and political salvation. Disillusionment with religious and political liberalism was so widespread in the United States during this decade that by the early 1970s Gallup polls revealed that Americans had reached "one of the lowest points of national morale in history."[22]

The failure of public and private institutions to perform what they promised in the 1960s eroded popular confidence in these institutions. This institutional failure was so devastating that it also undermined the confidence of individuals in their own personal behavior. Today, however, Americans increasingly divorce their individual self-confidence from their faith in economic, political, religious and social institutions.[23] Organized religion, for example, is an indispensable aspect of many Americans' relationship with God and the failure of religious institutions is a disappointment. But Americans "won't let that lowered esteem affect their own behavior."[24] Thus, although Christians in liberal Protestant churches may be disappointed with the spiritual emptiness of organized religion, they seek spiritual meaning elsewhere, often in the chrismatic renewal movement.

The growth in the number of pentecostal and charismatic Christians in the mainline Protestant and Catholic churches, in the classical pentecostal denominations and in independent, nondenominational churches since the beginning of the charismatic renewal movement in the late 1950s and early 1960s has been phenomenal. By 1980 nearly one-fifth of all adult Americans classified themselves as pentecostal or charismatic Christians.[25] The growth in the number of pentecostals and charismatics worldwide is even more phenomenal. In the mid-1980s Vinson Synan, the leading historian of American pentecostalism, cited projections that by the year 2000, 21% of the world's Christians would be charismatic or pentecostal.[26] However, the growth of the charismatic renewal has been so rapid that by 1991 pentecostals and charismatics already constitute one-fifth of Christians throughout the world.[27]

The Future of Charismatic Renewal

What is the future of the American charismatic movement? Unlike liberalism and to some extent evangelicalism, which have been part of the secularization of Christianity, the charismatic renewal movement is part of the "resacralization of religion."[28] Instead of conforming to the secular culture in which it exists, the charismatic movement has become more intentionally religious by deepening its spiritual commitment. The question is whether charismatics can maintain and strengthen this unique spiritual experience.

Religious movements in the past have suffered from the "routinization of charisma," a process first described by the German sociologist Max Weber in the early 1900s.[29] A social or religious movement which begins with inspired leadership often loses its magnetic appeal as its charisma becomes "routinized" and its organization becomes a bureaucracy. The routinization of charisma is a process of social development similar to the process of a sect becoming a church, which we described earlier with respect to American evangelicalism.

From the standpoint of secular history and sociology, if the new birth of charismatic renewal respects the pattern of its evangelical and pentecostal parents, the distinctive spiritual power of the charismatic movement is in mortal danger of surrendering to the seductive flattery of American secular culture and its impotent, hedonistic greed. However, from the standpoint of the Holy Spirit and of the Kingdom of God which, Jesus said, is already among or within us (Luke 17:21), the immediate future of charismatic revival is not predetermined. God is doing a new thing in the body of Christ, He is not restricted by the human weaknesses of the institutional churches, past or present, which act in His name. He is not bound by space or time and He will not be limited by our meager concepts of how Christ and culture interact or of how the history of the Christian Church instructs its future.

The Holy Spirit will not be satisfied with the charismatic renewal movement until God's complete and perfect purpose is accomplished in the Kingdom of God on earth. And in order for God's will to be done on earth as it is already done in heaven, charismatics must bring the spiritual power of their prophetic witness to bear upon all aspects and every part of the body of Christ. The charismatic renewal must not yield to the temptation of its evangelical and pentecostal heritage, the temptation of the warm and secure but spiritually deadly comfort of ministering only to individual souls and of obeying Christ' command to embody the Kingdom of God on earth by saving society one soul at a time. Nor must the charismatic movement submit to the equally tempting charms of the liberal mainline Protestant and Catholic churches whose prescription for social, economic and political salvation is painfully embarrassed by Christ's command to every human creature to confess Him and Him alone as Lord and Savior.

James D. G. Dunn identifies several models of Christian community in the New Testament. The "one-generation model" is the best model of Christian community for charismatic renewal because it is the most authetic model, the model closest to God's heart for His church. This model is not the church which organizes for the future, because

> the church which organises for the future may simply be ensuring that the future will be so burdened with the past that it cannot bring to reality Christian community in the present.[30]

If the charismatic renewal movement can maintain its spirit-filled "religious experience" against the manifold dangers of "the institutionalization of religion," then it will be an integral part of a new Great Awakening in America.[31] When charismatics proclaim the *whole* gospel and are neither embarrassed by openly preaching on the redemptive blood of Jesus nor offended by the radical, prophetic word to repent of our American sins of corporate greed, intolerable social and economic inequality and political corruption; then like the First Great Awakening in the late eighteenth century and the Second Great Awakening in the early nineteenth century, the charismatic movement can be the basis for "a new covenant vision" in the United States in the twenty-first century.[32]

Notes

1. Tocqueville, p. 291.
2. Swierenga, pp. 146-147.

3. Smith, p. 8.
4. Dayton, 1976, p. 99.
5. Moberg.
6. Hunter, 1987, p. 41.
7. Lovelace, p. 321.
8. Georgianna, pp. 265-267.
9. Dayton, 1976, pp. 1, 121-123.
10. Hunter, 1987, p. 48.
11. Smith, p. 203.
12. Lovelace, p. 376.
13. Smith, p. 188.
14. *Ibid.*, p. 191.
15. *Ibid.* , p. 195.
16. *Ibid.* , p. 219.
17. Robeck, pp. 103-107.
18. Beaman, p. 31.
19. Dempster, 1989, p. 59.
20. Beaman, p. 106.
21. Stafford, p. 36.
22. Gallup and Castelli, p. 11.
23. *Ibid.*, p. 44.
24. *Ibid.*
25. Kantzer, p. 25.
26. Synan, p. 44.
27. Chappell.
28. Poloma, 1982, p. 28.
29. Weber, pp. 363-373.
30. Dunn, p. 18.
31. Poloma, 1988, p. 246.
32. Rifkin, p. 241.

For Further Reading and Reflection

Readers interested in pacifism in the American pentecostal and holiness movements should consult Donald W. and Lucille S. Dayton, An Historical Survey of Attitudes Toward War and Peace Within the American Holiness Movement. This paper was presented to a Seminar on Christian Holiness and the Issues of War and Peace sponsored by the Commission on Social Action of the Christian Holiness Association and by the Peace and Social Concerns Commission of the Brethren in Christ, Winona Lake, Indiana, June 7 - 9, 1973.

For a different perspective on pentecostal pacifism in the United States see Murray W. Dempster, Reassessing the Moral Rhetoric of Early American Pentecostal Pacifism. *Crux*, vol. 26 (Mar. 1990) pp. 23-36. Dempster argues that the distinctive witness of American pentecostals was baptism in the Holy Spirit and the gifts of the Spirit. "Nowhere to my knowledge," he writes, "was pacifism ever integrated into this 'distinctive testimony' of the pentecostal outpouring of the Spirit." P. 32. See also Roger Robins, Our Forgotten Heritage: A Look At Early Pentecostal Pacifism. *Assemblies of God Heritage*, vol. 6 (Winter 1986-87), pp. 3-4.

In this chapter we have considered the relationship between evangelism and social reform in the United States in the nineteenth century. For an analysis of how nineteenth century American evangelism led to the social gospel see Brian Stanley, Evangelical Social and Political Ethics: An Historical Perspective. *The Evangelical Quarterly*, vol. 62 (Jan. 1990) pp. 19-36. Stanley writes, the "evangelical tradition was at least as important as more liberal theological influences in fashioning the rise of the social gospel movement." P. 27. See also David W. Bebbington, Evangelical Christianity and Modernism. *Crux*, vol. 26 (June 1990) pp. 2-9.

Why the evangelical tradition lost its original emphasis on social reform is, as we have said in this chapter, the subject of much scholarly debate. D. H. Battley, an Anglican priest from New Zealand and a leader in New Zealand's charismatic renewal movement, writes from an international perspective why charismatics are conservatives on matters of social reform. Charismatic Renewal: A View From Inside. *The Ecumenical Review*, vol. 38 (Jan. 1986) pp. 48-56. See especially pp. 54-56 of Battley's article.

In this chapter we have also discussed Donald Dayton's study of how American evangelicalism in the twentieth century has lost its emphasis on social reform. More recently, Dayton has written an article contrasting early nineteenth century evangelical social concern, which focused on fundamental institutional change, with late nineteenth century evangelical social concern, which focused on working within existing institutions. Pentecostalism in the United States, Dayton concludes, "emerged largely from the late nineteenth century revivalist ethos" with its emphasis on reform of existing socio-economic and political institutions. Pentecostal/Charismatic Renewal and Social Change: A Western Perspective. *Transformation: An International Dialogue On Evangelical Social Ethics*, vol. 5 (1988) p. 9.

To explain why American pentecostals lost their original concern with social and political issues, Jeffrey T. Snell states that the "disciplined and reordered lifestyles" of pentecostals "enabled them to rise economically and socially. The make-up of Pentecostalism had changed, and so had its identification with the social concerns and needs of those it left behind." Beyond the Individual and Into the World: A Call to Participation in the

Larger Purposes of the Spirit on the Basis of Pentecostal Theology. *Pneuma: The Journal of the Society for Pentecostal Studies*, vol. 14 (Spring 1992) p. 54.

Charles E. Jones has compiled a two volume, 9883-item annotated bibliography on the pentecostal movement entitled, *A Guide to the Study of the Pentecostal Movement*. It was published as Number 6 in the American Theological Library Association Bibliography Series by the Scarecrow Press (Metuchen, NJ) in 1983. In addition to documents, this bibliography contains the names and brief biographical information about hundreds of prominent pentecostal pastors.

Another bibliography, consisting of 2105 documents, which includes entries on both the pentecostal movement and the charismatic movement, is Watson E. Mills, *Charismatic Religion in Modern Research: A Bibliography. National Association of Baptist Professors of Religion Bibliographic Series*, No. 1. Macon, GA: Mercer University Press, 1985.

J. L. Packer has written two articles for *Christianity Today* on the charismatic movement. The first article, entitled, Charismatic Renewal, vol. 24 (Mar. 7, 1980), pp. 16-20, considers evangelical criticism of charismatics and discusses the strengths of the charismatic movement. The second article, entitled Piety on Fire, vol. 33 (May 12, 1989), pp. 18-23, defines the charismatic movement as a restrained, middle-class version of pentecostalism. Packer is also critical of the charismatic movement in this second article because, he says, the movement does not lead to full Christian maturity and persuades Christians to expect more from God than He has actually promised.

There are differences between evangelical and charismatic Christians in the United States. Corwin Smidt, writing in a sociology journal, reported that on questions of personal morality -- abortion, homosexuality, premarital sex, divorce and the use of alcohol -- "charismatics were consistently more 'liberal'" than evangelicals. "Praise the Lord" Politics: A Comparative Analysis of the Social Characteristics and Political Views of American Evangelical and Charismatic Christians. *Sociological Analysis*, vol. 50 (Spring 1988) p. 65. Smidt also found that a group he identifies as "charismatic evangelicals [to distinguish them from non-charismatic evangelicals] are more likely than other charismatics to stress evangelism, rather than communal and legislative efforts, as the top priority of Christians today." P. 71.

It is interesting to compare Smidt's results with the results of a 1979 survey of 36 Assembly of God district superintendents. These leaders of the largest classical pentecostal church in the United States stated that their lay members were not involved in political issues unless the issue was a question of personal morality, like the control of alcohol or homosexuality, or unless the issue involved the church as an institution, like textbook adoption in the public schools or government control of Christian schools. (Georgianna, 270-273).

One of the older works on the pentecostal and chaismatic movements is Michael P. Hamilton (ed.), *The Charismatic Movement*, Grand Rapids, MI: Eerdmans, 1975. This book includes an article by the Reverend Dennis J. Bennett, an Episcopal priest who began the charismatic renewal movement in mainline Protestant churches when, in 1960, he announced to his Van Nuys, California congregation that he had been filled with the Holy Spirit and spoke in tongues. The same book contains articles on black pentecostals and on how charismatic renewal impacts local churches.

Another older book, which is a historical survey of the pentecostal movement both in the United States and abroad, written by a scholar who is the son of a pentecostal minister, is John Thomas Nichol, *Pentecostalism.* New York: Harper & Row, 1966. In addition, Jorstad Erling (ed.), *The Holy Spirit in Today's Church: A Handbook of the New Pentecostalism* (Nashville and New York: Abingdon, 1973) is an overview of the charismatic renewal movement written for a popular audience. Also written for a popular audience is Sheila Macmanus Fahey, *Charismatic Social Action: Reflection/Resource Manual.* New York: Paulist Press, 1977. This book is a hands-on approach to social action for charismatics and other Christians with chapters devoted to the aged, correctional reform, drugs, the environment, hunger, poverty and race.

Peter D. Hocken, a Catholic charismatic from Great Britain, has written widely on the international charismatic movement. He has two entries -- Charismatic Communities, pp. 127-130 and Charismatic Movement, pp. 130-160 -- in the *Dictionary of Pentecostal and Charismatic Movements*, edited by Stanley M. Burgess and Gary B. McGee and published by Zondervan in Grand Rapids, MI in 1988.

Readers interested in the explosive growth of the charismatic movement in the United States among mainline Protestant, Catholic, classical pentecostal and non-denominational churches will want to see the *Christianity Today* reports on the 1987 New Orleans Conference of the North American Congress on the Holy Spirit and World Evangelization, What Does the Future Hold for Charismatic Renewal? which appeared in the May 16, 1986 issue (vol. 30), pp. 40, 41, 44; and The Holy Spirit and World Evangelization, which appeared in the September 4, 1987 issue (vol. 31) pp. 44-45.

An October 1988 nationwide Gallup survey of adult Americans found that 8% of the respondents describe themselves as pentecostal or charismatic. Among Protestants 12% identify themselves as pentecostal or charismatic, while 22% of evangelical Christians refer to themselves in this way. Only 4% of Catholics describe themselves as pentecostal or charismatic, but since the Roman Catholic Church is by far the largest single denomination in the United States with 28% of all Americans being members of the Catholic Church, there are 2.5 million Catholic charismatics in the United States. (Gallup and Castelli, 125-126).

The most dramatic growth in the pentecostal and charismatic movements, of course, is in Latin America, Africa and Asia. Walter J. Hollenweger, perhaps the leading authority on the international pentecostal and charismatic movements, predicts that by the year 2000 the number of charismatic and pentecostal Christians throughout the world will nearly equal the total number of all other Protestant Christians. (Hollenweger, 3).

At the very end of this chapter we quoted Jeremy Rifkin, who believes that the charismatic movement can be the basis for "a new covenant vision" in the United States comparable to the First Great Awakening in the eighteenth century and the Second Great Awakening in the early nineteenth century. According to James Davison Hunter a Third Great Awakening of the kind envisioned by Rifkin is "unlikely."

> A Third Great Awakening, or a Second Protestant Reformation as it has been called, with the same amount of influence as the First and Second Great Awakenings in America, or as the original Protestant Reformation, is a virtual sociological, not to mention legal, impossibility under the present conditions of modernity. (Hunter 1983, 133).

Chapter 2

An Assessment of the Charismatic Renewal Movement

> The body of Christ can only come to its full maturity when all the gifts of all its members reach full interplay with each other.
>
> -- Walter Hollenweger

Fifty years ago E. Stanley Jones, the great Christian missionary evangelist of the first half of the twentieth century, said that the "tragedy of American Christianity is that it has lost consciousness of its birthday, Pentecost."[1] "Pentecost," Jones wrote, is "normal Christianity."[2] But the American Church, he said, has inoculated itself and others with "a mild form of Christianity, so that it is now practically immune against the real thing."[3] Real Christianity, the Christianity that was revealed through the power of the Holy Spirit on the birthday of the Church at Pentecost, consists of two essential elements -- "purity for ourselves and power to impart the Message [of the Gospel of Jesus Christ] to others."[4]

The Contribution of the Charismatic Renewal Movement

These two elements which E. Stanley Jones identified as the permanent contribution of Pentecost to the Christian Church --

personal purity and evangelistic zeal to take the Good News to the ends of the earth -- also define the enduring legacy of the charismatic renewal movement. Today, in an age when American churches are more thoroughly secularized and more completely inoculated with mild Christianity than when Jones saw the need for a new Pentecost, the charismatic renewal movement has re-opened the Body of Christ to the person and power of the Holy Spirit and has thereby brought both personal spiritual transformation and a passion for evangelism to countless believers throughout the world. If the evangelical movement of the twentieth century established the objective revelation of God through the history of Israel in the Old Testament and through the birth, death and resurrection of Jesus Christ in the New Testament, then the charismatic renewal movement has established the subjective revelation of God in the souls of individual Christians through the power of God's Holy Spirit.[5]

According to Henry I. Lederle, a South African and a leading spokesman for the international charismatic movement, the charismatic renewal movement is probably "the most powerful religious awakening of the century."[6] The popularity and significance of charismatic renewal rests on its belief in a God who loves His human creatures personally and intimately, a God "you can feel, respond to, and love, [a] ... God who *cares* about our present and our future."[7] This openness to and faith in the creating and sustaining power of the Holy Spirit has revolutionized Christians throughout the world. Charismatic Christians have brought hope to a hopeless world, they have transformed lifeless worship into lively and explosive manifestations of signs and wonders and miracles through the presence of the Holy Spirit. Charismatics have turned prayers of meek petition into spiritual warfare and they have reversed the declining membership of the mainline Protestant churches by the exponential growth of charismatic and pentecostal congregations both within and independently of the established denominations. But does the charismatic renewal movement preach the whole gospel? Is it a gift which has blessed the whole body of Christ? If the charismatic movement has not blessed the whole Church, then "it is an aberration, a disharmonious interlude, which will have little lasting impact."[8]

The achievements of the charismatic renewal movement are prodigious. We have already spoken of the movement's recovery of the New Testament charismata or gifts of the Holy Spirit. Moreover, from the standpoint of the Christian churches, the charismatic renewal movement has, according to a popular spokesman for the evangelical movement, "earned respectability within the historic denominations and a place for the pentecostal experience in the religious mainstream."[9] However, the question remains, does charismatic renewal speak to the whole body of Christ? Does it preach the whole Gospel of Jesus Christ, including both personal and socio-political salvation? Do charismatics sometimes ignore the *fruit* of the Spirit, which after all are the purpose of the gifts and the only way in which to evaluate the gifts in terms of their strengthening the Body of Christ?

The Social and Political Witness of Charismatic Renewal

John R. W. Stott, a commentator and critic of the charismatic movement in Britain, emphasizes that the marks of a church renewed by the power of the Holy Spirit include not only sharing *in* the *koinonia* or fellowship of the Spirit but also sharing *out* of "our common gift to others" according to the prescription of Acts 2:44.[10] "The Christian community is the one community in the world in which poverty should be abolished."[11] Charismatic Christians who take the social witness of the Gospel seriously cannot tolerate "gross economic inequality within the Christian community."[12] Nor should charismatics permit economic inequality between rich and poor nations.

The charismatic renewal movement faces the question of its social, economic and political relevance not only in the United States, but throughout the world. Henry I. Lederle suggests four different approaches to social and political questions among charismatic Christians. The first approach is apolitical, maintaining complete separation of religion and politics, usually with implicit support for the status quo. In a later chapter on the weaknesses of both liberal and conservative American Christians we will discuss the sinful irresponsibility of this apolitical approach. The second approach of charismatics to socio-economic and political issues is the position of protesting against liberal positions only on issues of personal morality such as abortion, pornography and homosexuality. The third approach to involvement in social justice by charismatics is participation in "*mercy ministries*" or traditional charities like programs for the homeless, the unemployed and the hungry.[13] Finally, a growing number of charismatics are becoming involved in "*structural reform and systemic transformation*," for example, the nuclear freeze, the sanctuary movement and the protest against the shameful waste of scarce civilian resources on military extravagance.[14] This growing involvement of charismatic Christians in proclaiming the Kingdom of God to both individuals *and* institutions is not confined to the United States. In Latin America, which includes the nations with the largest numbers of pentecostal and charismatic Christians in the world, church leaders are moving rapidly toward more social and political involvement. Although the spiritual gifts proclaimed by the charismatic renewal movement must first be exercised in the life of the community of believers, if the community does not then exercise influence on the larger society, "it will be doomed to silence and thus to a lack of genuine love."[15] Latin American charismatics are learning that the pentecostal experience does not lead Christians "to withdraw from the world in which they live." Instead, pentecostal and charismatic Christians are being transformed by the Spirit to be "the instruments of God's intervention in that world."[16]

In Sweden, a European nation whose pentecostal-charismatic traditions are at least as old and as distinguished as the pentecostal-charismatic branch of the evangelical movement in the United States, Lewi Prethrus, the father of twentieth century Swedish pentecostalism, along with other pentecostal leaders in Sweden, founded the Christian Democratic Party in 1964. The impetus for the formation of the Swedish Christian Democratic Party was the widespread and accelerating secularization of Swedish culture and society and the belief of the Party's pentecostal leadership that Christian values should be preserved through political action. Prethrus himself supported the Conservative Party of Sweden in the 1950s, but led the movement to organize the Christian Democratic Party when he became disillusioned with the position of the Conservatives on questions of personal morality, a position which he considered to be too liberal.[17] Like a majority of American pentecostals and charismatics, who are politically conservative, Swedish pentecostals identify the sin of relativism and secularism, which have grown from liberal Protestant theology, with political liberalism. In Western Europe and the United States pentecostals and charismatics are therefore politically conservative and focus their social concern on questions of individual morality like abortion and homosexuality. On the other hand, in the two-thirds world pentecostals and charismatics focus their social concern on questions of institutional and corporate morality like economic development and political inequality.

"Why do Christians with similar spiritual experience come to such different political conclusions?"[18] Certainly the history and contemporary secular culture of the various Christian nations help explain why Christians today do not have the spiritual unity which Jesus prayed in John 17:20-23 that both his disciples and those who were converted by his disciples would have. But we do not know the complete explanation for such diversity among charismatic and pentecostal Christians on socio-economic and political issues. However, we do know from Jesus' prayer to God that unity among Christians is necessary "in order that the world may know that you sent me and that you love them [Jesus' disciples and those who believed the disciples' message] as you love me." (John 17:23TEV). True spiritual ecumenism is thus the key to evangelism. The Gospel of Jesus Christ will not be believed by those who have not heard it until and unless Christians are "one" just as Jesus and his heavenly Father are "one."

Charismatic Renewal and Ecumenism

Unity among so many different Christians in so many widely dispersed nations with so many different social, economic and political issues is only possible through the power of the Holy Spirit. And pentecostals and charismatics, whose precious gift to the Body of Christ is based on their rediscovery of the Holy Spirit, must be especially sensitive to how the Holy Spirit is bringing unity to the Church. American pentecostals and charismatics see the world-wide evangelical power of the Holy Spirit in the fact that by the year 2000 charismatic and pentecostal Christians throughout the world will nearly equal the total number of all other Protestants. However, American pentecostals and charismatics should be equally aware that by the end of the century the geographical center of Christianity "will shift away from white western" nations. "Christianity as a whole will no longer be a predominantly white person's religion."[19]

As the geographic and demographic center of Christianity shifts from the first world to the two-thirds world, American evangelicals, including pentecostals and charismatics, must broaden the scope of their ethical emphasis from questions of personal morality like abortion and homosexuality, which concern primarily North American and Western Europe, to global issues like hunger and the gross maldistribution of the world's economic resources, which concern primarily the two-thirds world. By becoming more aware of and more sensitive to these issues, which have top priority among the emerging majority of all Christians in Asia, Africa and Latin America, American pentecostals and charismatics can more nearly approach the unity which Jesus prayed for in John 17 and they can evangelize more effectively by teaching the Good News to "all nations" and by being Jesus' witnesses "unto the uttermost part of the earth." (Matthew 28:20; Luke 1:8KJV).

Moreover, the quest for unity among the Body of Christ must not stop with the Christian Church. Arnold Bittlinger, one of the most well known British leaders of the international charismatic movement, points out that the "Spirit of God is also at work outside the people of God."[20] Using Jesus' response to John's question about those who cast out devils in Jesus' name but were not among Jesus' twelve disciples: "whoever is not against us is for us" (Mark 9:40TEV), Bittlinger calls for a truly ecumenical and evangelical charismatic experience which will reach all of the world's people and embrace them all in the Kingdom of God.

How can all of the world's people identify themselves as the children of God in His Kingdom? The process begins in each nation with the discovery of those things which inhibit Christian unity and divide the body of Christ. In the United States, as we explained in Chapter 2, the most spiritually divisive faction, the fissure which is most grievous to the Holy Spirit, is the separation between liberal and conservative Christians, between liberal Christians who emphasize social, economic and political justice and conservative pentecostal and charismatic Christians who merely focus on salvation of the individual. We turn now to a consideration of the weaknesses of both of these streams of American Christianity.

Notes

1. Jones, 1944, p. 232.
2. *Ibid.*, 1925, p. 157.
3. *Ibid.*, pp. 126-127.
4. *The Theology and Missiology of E. Stanley Jones*, p. 35.
5. Dods, p. 72.
6. Lederle, p. 62.
7. Davis, p. 107.
8. *Ibid.*, p. 103.

9. Quebedeaux, 1983, p. 236.
10. Stott, p. 18.
11. *Ibid.*, p. 19.
12. *Ibid.*
13. Lederle, pp. 68-69.
14. *Ibid.*, p. 69.
15. Petrella, p. 36.
16. *Ibid.*, p. 37, emphasis deleted.
17. Sahlberg, pp. 27-29.
18. *Ibid.*, p. 29.
19. Hollenweger, p. 3.
20. Bittlinger, p. 122.

For Further Reading and Reflection

In the first pages of this chapter we explored the astonishing spiritual achievements of the charismatic renewal movement. It would be interesting to trace the use of the nine gifts of the Spirit listed by Paul in I Corinthians 12:8-10 -- *wisdom, knowledge, faith, healing, miracles, prophecy, discerning of spirits, speaking in tongues and the interpretation of tongues* -- throughout the history of the Church. British Bible scholar Ronald A. N. Kydd has begun to research this history of the use of the gifts of the Holy Spirit by describing the church's practice of the gifts from the time of Christ's resurrection to the year 320 A. D. Kydd states that "New Testament Christianity was charismatic. Times when the Holy Spirit broke in upon them with great force were common to these Christians." *Charismatic Gifts in the Early Church.* Peabody, MA: Hendrickson, 1984, p. 1. However, the early church was "strongly charismatic" only until about 200 A. D. P. 4.

What happened in 200 A. D. to undermine the exercise of the gifts? One clue to the mystery is the events of 320 A. D., events which mark a radical and cataclysmic change in the history of the Church. In that year -- 320 A. D. -- the Roman Emperor Constantine became a Christian convert and Christianity became the officially established religion of the Roman Empire. E. Stanley Jones puts the matter succinctly. "What ... happened was that the Christian Church had been conquered by a pagan warrior." (Jones, 1931, p. 13). A spiritual decay must have been at work in the Body of Christ between 200 and 320 A. D. in order for it to be conquered and held captive by Constantine and by the political and military power of Rome. The declining use of the gifts of the Spirit after 200 A. D. is symptomatic of this spiritual decay.

With respect to charismatic renewal and ecumenism, Peter Hocken, a Roman Catholic charismatic and a leading historian of the charismatic renewal movement in Great Britain and elsewhere, has written that "the charismatic renewal is of its nature ecumenical and that it is a grace of God for the reunification of His people." Charismatic Renewal and Christian Unity. *America*, vol. 141, Dec. 1, 1979, p. 340. In a similar vein James Robison, the Texas evangelist, stated that, "Whoever has the heart of God wants the whole church to be brought together in true spiritual oneness." (Nov. 30, 1988, television broadcast, WHMB, Channel 40, Indianapolis, Indiana).

Garry D. Nation, writing in *Christianity Today*, identifies James Robison as the founder of "charismatic restorationism." P. 27. Moreover, Nation says that "[w]e find the direct ancestors for the charismatic restorationists of today in the early Pentecostal movement." P. 28. The Restoration Movement. *Christianity Today*, vol. 36 (May 18, 1992) pp. 27-31.

Walter J. Hollenweger, the dean of the international charismatic movement who was quoted at the very beginning of this chapter, has said that the ecumenicity of the pentecostal and charismatic movements lies in their religious practice, not in their doctrine or theology. Pentecostals and the Charismatic Movement. *The Study of Spirituality*, ed. Cheslyn Jones, Geoffrey Wainwright and Edward Yarnold. New York and Oxford: Oxford University Press, 1986, pp. 553-554.

Moreover, Cardinal Leon Joseph Suenens, writing to other Catholics, offers requirements for both "authentic ecumenism" and "authentic charismatic renewal" as well as pastoral guidelines for local churches and parishes. *Ecumenism and Charismatic Renewal: Theological and Pastoral Orientations. Malines Document* 2. London: Darton, Longman & Todd, 1978.

The charismatic and pentecostal movements clearly provide a rich and solid theological basis for ecumenism among all Christians, from the most unwavering fundamentalist to the most radical proponent of liberation theology. However, the difficulties of actually achieving unity among such diverse Christians should not be underestimated. See the recent work of the brilliant South African theologian, Henry I. Lederle, now at Oral Roberts University. The Pentecostal and Charismatic Movements: An Ambiguous Renewal of the Christian Church? *Ministerial Formation*, no. 50 (July 1990) pp. 35-43; and The Spirit of Unity: A Discomforting Comforter. *Ecumenical Review*, vol. 42 (July - October 1990) pp. 279-287.

Near the beginning of this chapter we noted a number of efforts by European and African church leaders to involve the charismatic movement in social and political issues. In this regard see Raymond Pfister, Some Reflections on Social Ministry in European Pentecostal Churches: Three Case Studies. *EPTA Bulletin: Bulletin of the European Pentecostal Theolo-*

gical Association, vol. 10 (1991) pp. 19-24.

Chapter 3

Weaknesses of Liberals and Conservatives

Over the course of the past two decades political and religious liberalism has lost most of its authority to shape "public moral discourse" in America.[1] Protestant liberalism in particular is no longer generally recognized as a decisive influence either in determining the proper role of public institutions in American society or in defining their relationship to each other. Richard John Neuhaus, who has written widely on the relationship of religion to social, economic and political institutions in the United States, states that "the leadership in religion's culture-forming tasks" has passed from Protestant liberals to "evangelicals and Roman Catholics."[2]

Is Liberalism Obsolete?

There are a number of reasons for American liberalism's loss of cultural influence. In the Introduction to this book we traced contemporary Protestant liberalism to its source in nineteenth century American intellectual history. Liberalism was a largely successful effort to accommodate the Christian faith to a secular culture which was at that time intensely optimistic about the human benefits of applying scientific methods to almost all private and public institutions. Today, however, when Americans are more sceptical about scientific "progress" and more aware of the human, ecological and spiritual costs of the application of scientific methods, Protestant liberalism seems to be out of date. Christianity is now seeking not to identify itself with, but to distinguish itself from, American secular culture.

Another reason for the apparent failure of Protestant liberalism in the United States is its endorsement of pluralism and relativism. In an article entitled, "Does Liberal Protestantism Have An American Future?" William R. Hutchison, one of the leading spokesmen for religious liberalism, states that what American Christianity needs is a "positive theology of pluralism."[3] The problem is that if pluralism rests on the assumption that the Christian faith is merely one of many expressions of religious truth, then Christianity has no unique claim to divine revelation. All claims to divine inspiration are relative. Without the certainty of God's revelation of Himself to man through the Old and New Testaments and without the assurance of the Gospel that Jesus Christ is the only Son of God who was crucified and resurrected to atone for all human sin and to reconcile all mankind to God, Christianity loses its credibility.

Still another weakness of liberalism is its association with political extremism, especially liberation theology. Liberation theology has the reputation of being Marxism baptized with a little superficial Christianity. According to a Review Essay in the *Journal for the Scientific Study of Religion* liberation theology in many cases puts political and economic liberation of the poor first and theology second.[4] However, liberation theology is more than "Marxism in Christian disguise."[5] H. Mark Roelofs, a political scientist, writes that liberation theology is the rediscovery of a "profound biblical political radicalism" whose roots are in the New Testament gospels and in the book of Acts.[6] The principles which emerge from this interpretation of the Christian Gospel are "radical egalitarianism ... radical communitarianism ... [and] radical pacifism."[7]

In a later chapter, One in Mind and Spirit, which integrates the spiritual revelations of the pentecostal-charismatic movement with the scriptural truths of the liberal social justice stream of American Christianity, we will return to some of these aspects of liberation theology. At this point, however, liberation theology is associated with a weakness of religious liberalism because it is an emotionally supercharged code-word for many conservative Christians in the United States and because it is a source of bitter acrimony within the body of Christ. If the Gospel of Jesus Christ is especially the Gospel of the poor, as liberation theology claims, did not Jesus also bring Good News to the bourgeoisie and the rich? Does not liberation theology run afoul of Paul's admonition against "divisions" in the church? (I Corinthians 11:18KJV).

Liberation theology is not the only source of divisiveness associated with liberal Christianity. The ordination of homosexuals as clergy; the substitution of gender neutral language like "Creator, Redeemer and Sustainer" for the traditional "Father, Son and Holy Spirit"; and the economic boycott of multi-national corporations like Shell Oil Company because they did not completely withdraw from South Africa before the official end of apartheid, have all become issues as divisive if not more divisive than liberation theology within and among American mainline Protestant churches. The adoption or proposed adoption of controversial positions on these and other highly inflammatory issues have galvanized conservative mainline Protestants to take positions like those described in the United Methodist Houston Declaration of 1988 to reaffirm traditional doctrines.[8] Other mainline churches in the United States have become embroiled in similar situations.

International ecumenical bodies like the World Council of Churches are just as controversial as some American Protestant churches. C. L. Patijn, writing in *The Ecumenical Review*, a publication of the World Council of Churches, states that under the WCC "the agenda of the world has bcome the agenda of the Church." Not only churches in the United States but churches throughout the world "have been carried away by too many political and cultural short-term concerns and by too many new urgencies in social action."[9] In the words of Scottish moral philosopher Gordon Graham, "[t]here is a regrettable tendency for modern Christian theology to be bandwagon theology."[10] Whenever a belief or cause becomes fashionable among middle class intellectuals, Christian theologians jump on the bandwagon and provide a Christian justification for the belief or cause.

Perhaps it is time for liberalism to receive "the grace of doing nothing." These words appear as the title to an editorial in *The Christian Century*. The editorial is based on the "only published disagreement" between Reinhold and his brother H. Richard Niebuhr. The dispute appeared in a March 1932 issue of *The Christian Century* with respect to the Japanese invasion of Manchuria. H. Richard Niebuhr, taking issue with his brother, advised doing nothing in some circumstances as an act of personal repentance, that is, taking the log out of one's own eye before accusing another of having a splinter in his eye. H. Richard also counseled doing nothing as an act of faith in God's redemptive purposes in history and, at least in some cases, as a better Christian witness than taking bold and decisive action. Applying

Richard Niebuhr's advice to contemporary American churches, the editorial suggests that the grace of doing nothing means to refrain "from participating in the multitude of Christian social-action paths and their resulting protests and demands."[11]

The Hypocrisy of Conservative Christianity

If Protestant liberals in the United States have sinned by baptizing various left-wing secular ideologies as Christian, then religious conservatives, ironically, have sinned by baptizing *their* ideologies, especially laissez faire capitalism and representative democracy modeled on the contemporary American examples of these economic and political institutions, as Christian. Evangelical, pentecostal and charismatic Christians in the United States are usually classified as religious and political conservatives. The weakness of evangelicals, pentecostals and charismatics in giving divine sanction to corporate greed and to egregious social and economic inequality at home and to American political and cultural imperialism abroad is the counterpart of the mainline liberal Protestant weakness described above.

There are several reasons for the American evangelical, pentecostal, and charismatic endorsement of the social, economic and political status quo in the United States. We have already examined the nineteenth century history of American evangelicalism which combined personal salvation with social reform. And we have considered how twentieth century evangelicals, pentecostals and charismatics have abandoned social reform and focused almost exclusively on the redemption of individual souls. Why have contemporary American Christian conservatives continued to reject responsibility for institutional change?

One of the most frequently expressed conservative criticisms of liberal mainline Protestant churches is that these churches should leave politics to the politicans and stick to preaching the gospel and saving souls. Mainline Protestant laymen who make this criticism about their own and other churches are political conservatives who disagree with the liberalism of these churches' clergy and administrative hierarchy. Sometimes those who say that politics and religion should be separate and mutually exclusive areas of human concern provide biblical justification for their position.

Political scientist Claes Ryn, for example, says that "it is not expected of the statesman that he should take no thought for the morrow or turn the other cheek in the conduct of his duties."[12] The statesman is not exempt from Jesus' commandments because his secular responsibilities cannot be part of the Kingdom of God but because, as a personally committed Christian, the statesman must protect the institutions for which he is a trustee against those who are not Christian. A similar argument has been made by Marte Tilton, wife of Texas televangelist Robert Tilton. She believes that the United States cannot risk nuclear disarmament. "To disarm our country of powerful weapons is like telling the devil you will give up your power over him if he will just leave you in peace." Neither the devil nor "the enemies of this country" will "leave us in peace."[13]

There are several problems with this line of conservative argument. To say that Christian churches have little or no obligation to redress economic and political conditions in the United States or abroad is spiritually irresponsible. Even though the Church is a fallible human institution and will never fully embody the Kingdom of God until Jesus Christ returns to earth, it dare not fail to denounce and use all its spiritual and physical resources to correct all evil which it confronts, both individual and corporate. The body of Christ today must identify the obscene accumulation of both conventional and nuclear weapons by all nations as sin. And it must through prayer and through the responsible use of its citizenship do everything it can to end the use and ultimately the existence of these weapons. Either "the weapons of our warfare" are carnal as conservatives claim or, as Paul says in I Corinthians 10:4, they are "not carnal."

Another problem with the conservative argument that politics and religion should be kept separate and distinct is the responsibility of individual Christians to a sick and sinful world. Just as the Church, which is the body of Christ in the world, has a corporate responsibility to overcome evil with good, so individual Christians are called to take the Gospel not only to other persons in need of salvation but also to economic, social and political institutions which are equally in need of redemption. The statesman and the businessman and the president of a civic club who do not apply biblical principles in the conduct of their duties betray their commitment to the Gospel and leave the government, the corporation and the club without the guiding light of Jesus Christ. The conservative separation of religion from politics and from other secular affairs means that Christians sanction and participate in behavior and structures which are not only indifferent to but are actually hostile to the Gospel of Jesus Christ.

Conservative American Christians, especially evangelicals in recent years, are recognizing the necessity of addressing social and political as well as personal sin. Terry Muck, for example, writing in *Christianity Today*, offers guidelines for how evangelical Christians, unaccustomed to political protest, should select an institutional grievance and conduct an effective campaign to remedy the grievance. The first question, Muck suggests, is whether the issue is sufficiently serious in terms of theology, in terms of immediate danger and in terms of long-range consequences to justify the resources necessary to correct the problem. The second question is whether the goals of the protest are reasonable and whether they are clearly stated. Third, will the protest be effective and will there be any side effects? Finally, protestors should ask what long-range results will follow their action.[14] Evangelical Christians are to be commended for being more responsible in broadening the scope of their concern from individual sins like abortion, homosexuality and pornography to economic and political sins like inequalities in income and social status, hunger in the United States and abroad and corporate greed.

Hoever, as we will demonstrate in a later chapter -- One in Mind and Spirit -- the ethical principle of choosing means which are necessary and sufficient to achieve a Christian end, whether employed by liberals or conservatives, is not the morality of the Kingdom of God as proclaimed by Jesus Christ. From the standpoint of the Kingdom of God means *are* ends. The Kingdom is so radical that means and ends occur simultaneously. No evil no matter how small or how closely related to the greatest possible good can ever be justified on the basis of Gospel of the Kingdom.

Another prominent American evangelical who has acknowledged the problem he and his fellow evangelicals have with social and political issues is the Christian social ethicist Richard J. Mouw. In many cases, Mouw believes, conservative Christians permit their insistence on the exclusive authority of the Bible to become dogmatic insistence on the ideologies of fundamentalism and Biblical inerrancy. What is needed, according to Mouw, is greater recognition among evangelicals of the important role of plurality in the Church -- a plurality that is not merely relativism.[15]

Finally, Carl F. H. Henry, the dean of conservative Christian theologians in the United States, thinks that the problem with American evangelicals and other conservative Christians is that they have had a private, partisan political agenda. Conservative Christians lack a public philosophy of the common good. The New Christian

Right, in particular, is suspected by other Christians and non-Christians of wanting to pursue its agenda at their expense and of wanting to impose its vision of a Christian polity on everyone else. Henry calls for a Christian public philosophy among evangelicals.[16] "Nothing precludes an interreligious or ecumenical cooperative public witness against injustice or for justice." Moreover, Henry proposes that American evangelicals take the initiative in establishing this public witness "because we so easily forfeit the initiative to others."[17]

Both liberals and conservatives among American Protestants fall short of the Kingdom of God. Liberalism, which began as a form of Christian accommodation to the late nineteenth century gospel of wealth and material progress, has become almost obsolete in an age of economic scarcity and environmental catastrophes. Liberals, moreover, by making a virtue of tolerance for religious diversity, have yielded to the temptation of a pluralism which is too often only the ancient sin of idolatrous relativism. It is time for liberals to pull back from their socio-political agendas and to rediscover both the redemptive power of Jesus' death and resurrection and the correcting and reassuring presence of the Holy Spirit.

Both liberals and conservatives must stop consecrating their separate political agendas as the uniquely definitive Christian voice on these issues. In addition, conservative Christians in the United States, including evangelical, pentecostal and charismatic Christians, are especially prone to the sin of sanctifying only questions of personal morality while ignoring and thereby tacitly promoting the equally sinful socio-economic and political status quo. A growing number of conservative Christians are recognizing the hypocrisy of this false and blatantly un-Scriptural dichotomy between the individual and society. As these conservatives begin to move away from the doctrinaire legalism of early twentieth century fundamentalism and reach out to moderate and liberal American Christians, we pray that liberals in their turn, who have bravely spearheaded ecumenism in the past, will reach out to their evangelical, pentecostal and charismatic brothers and sisters in Christ and discover again "the unity of the Spirit in the bond of peace" (Ephesians 4:3KJV) which is absolutely indispensable for the proclamation of the present reality of the Kingdom of God.

Notes

1. Neuhaus, p. 672.
2. *Ibid.*
3. Hutchison, p. 10.
4. Levine, pp. 555-556.
5. Roelofs, p. 549.
6. *Ibid.*, p. 550.
7. *Ibid.*, p. 554.
8. Duin, pp. 51-52.
9. Patijn, p. 368.
10. Graham, p. 21.
11. Kelley, p. 941.
12. Ryn, p. 121.
13. Tilton, p. 14.
14. Muck, pp. 14-15.
15. Mouw, pp. 366-367.
16. Henry, pp. 26-27.
17. *Ibid.*, p. 28.

For Further Reading and Reflection

Richard John Neuhaus, cited at the very beginning of this chapter, describes himself as "religiously orthodox, culturally conservative, politically liberal and economically pragmatic." (Neuhaus, p. 669). He is best known for his book *The Naked Public Square* which reflects both his religious orthodoxy and his political liberalism. This book is an effort to restore liberalism's lost faith in the power and beneficent potential of public authority by establishing "a new moral consensus based on Biblical religion." (Fox, p. 8).

A similar book by Robert N. Bellah and four of his colleagues, *Habits of the Heart: Individualism and Commitment in American Life*, published by Harper and Row in 1985, proposes the reestablishment of a secular tradition of "communal discourse" to replace the dominant but empty and exhausted rhetoric of "expressive individualism," which is the very heart and soul of political and religious liberalism in the United States. In 1991 Bellah and his colleagues extended their argument for the creation of genuine community in the United States by providing a specific moral and philosophical context for community in our economic, political, legal, educational and religious institutions. *The Good Society*. New York: Vintage Books, 1992.

These two books -- *The Naked Public Square* and *Habits of the Heart* -- have attracted enormous public attention, far beyond the academic circles of the social sciences and religious studies, because they penetrate the spiritual depth of America's crisis of public authority so incisively. One commentator, Lucy Bregman, suggests that charismatic Christianity may help resolve the dilemma of expressive individualism which cannot transcend individual self-interest to embrace larger communities. Two Imageries of Peace: Popular Psychology and Charismatic Christianity. *Horizons*, vol. 16. (Spring 1989) pp. 79-96.

Charismatic Christianity also has much to offer to individual public officials. Instead of being spiritual schizophrenics as suggested in this chapter by political scientist Claes Ryn, Arnold Bittlinger, the British leader of the international charismatic movement, writes that the church must support its members "who assume ... responsible positions in economic and political life, so that they may speak God's word and do God's deeds even in difficult situations and thereby work together so that God's salvation and healing may come to our sick world." (Bittlinger, p. 122).

In this chapter we also referred to a disagreement between the brothers Reinhold and H. Richard Niebuhr over whether the United States should have intervened when the Japanese invaded Manchuria in 1932. It would be interesting to compare more precisely what each of the two brothers thought the United States should do in response to this international crisis. As the two outstanding American liberal Christian theologians of the twentieth century the Niebuhrs' positions on American foreign policy during the mid-1930s is particularly relevant to the Christian moral dilemmas of our foreign policy today, because it was the United States which sold to Japan the arms it used to invade Manchuria. On the general issue of how Christians should respond to their nation's foreign policy see John C. Bennett, *Foreign Policy In Christian Perspective*. New York: Charles Scribner's Sons, 1966.

The relationship between religion and politics in the United States is usually expressed as the relationship between church and state. George M. Marsden, one of the leading authorities on church-state relations in the United States, identifies two traditions of American church-state relations. The first tradition is a tradition formed by the struggle for secular political power in the early years of the American republic. This was a tradition "shaped by a dissenting Protestant and Enlightenment coalition against Anglican political power in the colonies." Afterword, Religion, Politics, and the Search for an American Consensus. *Religion and American Politics: From the Colonial Period To the 1980s*, ed. Mark A. Noll. New

York: Oxford University Press, 1990, p. 381.

The other tradition of American church-state relations, according to Marsden, is Puritanism. As compared with the first tradition, which rested on a balance of secular political power, Puritanism requires "a more integral relationship between Christianity and public life." P. 382. While the secular tradition has determined the political, and especially the legal and judicial, perspective on church-state relations in the United States, Puritanism, from its Christian perspective on American church-state relations, has influenced both the eighteenth century Great Awakening and the Second Great Awakening of the first half of the nineteenth century.

The charismatic renewal movement is either the last movement of the Second Great Awakening or the first movement of a Third Great Awakening. In either case, from the standpoint of the two traditions of American church-state relations, the question is whether the charismatic renewal movement points toward a new Puritanism in church-state relations.

Chapter 4

Repentance and Renewal

> It is passing strange that we in the Christian community,
> which proclaims the inexhaustible mercy of God,
> fear admitting our mistakes and confessing our sins.
>
> --Richard John Neuhaus

What can bring American charismatics and pentecostals together with the advocates of liberalism and social justice? The kind of reconciliation between these groups which will bring about the renewal of the Church begins with repentance. John the baptizer in the first century A. D. prepared the way for Jesus Christ by preaching repentance. Repentance is still part of twentieth century American Christianity, but it is interpreted in different ways by different groups within the Church. American evangelicals, including pentecostals and charismatics, interpret repentance as renunciation of sin leading to the conversion and salvation of the individual sinner. Christians who advocate liberal social justice, on the other hand, do not deny that each person must confess his sins and accept Jesus Christ for himself as his personal savior. But they insist that personal salvation is not the whole Gospel. Liberal social justice advocates believe that the Body of Christ must proclaim the Good News not only to individuals but also to all the human stuructures and social institutions which need the explosive, redeeming power of Jesus Christ.

The Need for Individual and Collective Repentance

We believe that agreement on the need for both personal and corporate repentance by both charismatics and pentecostals and by advocates of liberal social justice is the key to their reconciliation within the Body of Christ. The evangelical theologian Richard Lovelace recognizes this necessity for "*comprehensive repentance*" among American Christians as the prerequisite for both personal and social redemption.[1] Lovelace recommends the three-fold pattern of repentance first proclaimed by the Old Testament prophets: "the rejection of idolatry or false religion; the renunciation of adultery, drunkenness and other personal sins; and a renewal of caring for the poor and needy, forsaking indifference, fighting oppression and seeking justice."[2]

From the standpoint of disunity in the American Church the greatest sin of both liberals and pentecostals and charismatics is idolatry. These groups permit their own traditions and doctrines to take the place of God Himself. Instead of worshipping God in the name of Jesus Christ, the advocates of liberal social justice as well as charismatics and pentecostals worship God in the name of their interpretation of Jesus Christ. Moreover, each group accuses the other of unfaithfulness to the Gospel because the two groups do not have the same interpretation of Jesus Christ.

Liberals, for example, accuse charismatics and pentecostals of supporting an unjust and iniquitous status quo by their failure to attack racism. Thomas Soeldner, a missionary of the Evangelical Lutheran Church in America to the Methodist Church of South Africa, criticized the charismatic churches in South Africa at a time when the South African government was pursuing an official policy of apartheid. Charismatic churches in South Africa, Soeldner wrote, "embrace an individualized Christianity and an individual salvation" which are consistent with the South African government's "social and economic individualism."[3]

American charismatics and pentecostals, on the other hand, criticize liberals for neglecting the primacy of personal salvation and for substituting their own social and political views for New Testament doctrine. In addition to criticizing the advocates of liberal social justice, charismatics and pentecostals also criticize and are criticized by evangelicals. Robert Booth Fowler, a political scientist and leading scholar of the evangelical movement, states that even though American pentecostals and charismatics are part of the evangelical movement in the United States, evangelicals have often been sharply critical of pentecostals and charismatics.[4] Evangelicals question the pentecostal and charismatic belief that all the gifts of the Spirit discussed by Paul in I Corinthians 12 are available to Christians today just as much as they were available to the New Testament Church. Responding to this criticism by evangelicals, charismatics and pentecostals accuse evangelicals of legalism, of exalting the letter over the spirit of God's Word and of rendering the Holy Spirit impotent by splitting hairs over irrelevant theologies like Biblical inerrancy and dispensationalism while completely ignoring the person and the power of Jesus Christ.

All of these criticisms -- the liberal accusation that evangelicals participate in institutional sins by failing to proclaim a prophetic witness against them; the evangelical (including pentecostal and charismatic) judgment against liberals for baptizing their own socio-economic and political opinions as *the* Word from God for the American Church; the evangelical critique of pentecostals and charismatics that their belief in the continuing power of the spiritual gifts is not Scripturally sound; and the pentecostal and charismatic reply to evangelicals that their doctrines are like arguing about how many angels can dance on the head of a pin while hundreds of millions of souls throughout the world are desperately crying out for salvation -- are rooted not in the values of Jesus Christ but in the cultural values of the various churches and denominations in the United States. To quote Richard Quebedeaux, the popular evangelical writer, culture "is not inherently evil." But when "cultural values take priority over the values of Jesus in the life of a Christian," then they become "an idol, and must be rejected."[5]

The Scriptural Basis for Personal and Corporate Repentance

It is time for Christians to stop confessing each other's sins and begin confessing their own sins. All Christians in the United States, whether liberal or conservative or evangelical or pentecostal or charismatic, must first take the splinters out of their own eyes before they accuse other Christians of having logs in their eyes. Guilt and sorrow for sin are universal human reactions to transgressing the law which God has placed in every human heart. But only Jesus Christ, the Son of God, could turn sorrow for sin into gladness.

In his second letter to the Corinthians Paul refers to his sometimes sharp criticism of the Corinthian Church in an earlier letter. Paul's rebuke, however, did not cause insurmountable guilt or the "sadness which is merely human" among the Corinthian Christians. Rather, Paul's harsh words created "the sadness that is used by God" to bring "a change of heart that leads to salvation." (II Corinthians 7:10TEV).

Here in microcosm is the whole Gospel of Jesus Christ. Paul speaks directly to the chastened Corinthians in the first person singular, "I take such pride in you! ... I am running over with joy." (II Corinthinans 7:4TEV). Paul is witnessing and testifying to a literal resurrection of the Corinthian Church after its sin had produced a sorrow, which, had it been "merely human," would have caused irreversible death. But Paul is writing about and proclaiming a resurrected Savior who has already defeated death, not only in His own human body but also for every person and every other part of the Body of Christ, whether individual or corporate, which confesses its sin and accepts Jesus Christ as its eternal Lord.

This is the confession and resurrection which both liberal Christians and charismatic and pentecostal Christians in the United States need -- repentance which, in the words of James F. Breckenridge writing in *Decision* magazine, published by the Billy Graham Evangelisitic Association, causes us to "become rebels against sin rather than against God."[6] Our rebellion against sin will never be completed in our human bodies in this life. But as Christians committed to do the work of the Kingdom of God on earth we are called to be perfect and to remove completely any and all sources of disunity within the Body of Christ. Just as Christ conditions the Father's forgiveness of our personal trespasses on our forgiveness of those who have individually trespassed against us (Matthew 6:12), so God will not forgive the advocates of liberal social justice or the pentecostals or charismatics until and unless they forgive the group in the Church which has offended or injured them.

Corporate repentance is just as important and has just as much Scriptural foundation as individual repentance. Throughout the book of Leviticus Moses prescribes in great detail the rules and regulations for Israel's offerings and sacrifices to God. In Leviticus 4 Moses tells the Hebrews what offerings they should make to God for unintentional sins. And in verses 13-21 of Leviticus 4 Moses states what must be done "[i]f it is the whole community of Israel that sins and becomes guilty of breaking one of the Lord's commands without intending to."

(Leviticus 4:13TEV).

Similarly, in the New Testament Letter from James, the author addresses the Christian community and admonishes his readers to practice collective repentance among themselves, not merely individual repentance to God. "So then, confess your sins to one another and pray for one another." (James 5:16TEV). Moreover, James commands his fellow believers, "Do not criticize one another." (James 4:11TEV). The Christian who judges another Christian usurps what only God can do. "Who do you think you are, to judge your fellow-man?" (James 4:12TEV). To presume to judge a fellow Christian is in fact both blasphemy and idolatry because the Christian who judges another Christian not only sets himself above God, he uses and therefore worships some law other than God's law. And only God, of course, can apply God's law to human beings with justice and equity.

Other Examples of Corporate Repentance

American Christians are not the only Christians to identify personal and corporate repentance as the absolutely indispensable prerequisite for the restoration of true unity within the Body of Christ. Archbishop Kirill of Smolensk and Vyazma in the Russian Orthodox Church sees repentance not only as the key to unity among Christians but also as the key to the renewal of all humanity, both Christian and non-Christian. He says, "Repentance -- metanoia -- is transformation of the old order of life and spirit; it is the realization of untruth and its rejection; it is *perestroika* in the deepest sense of the word."[7]

As Christians anywhere in the world we can even learn God's lesson of repentance from non-Christians. E. Stanley Jones, the most outstanding Methodist of at least the first half of the twentieth century, who is best remembered today as a missionary evangelist to India, was a personal friend of Gandhi. After Gandhi's death, which, Jones writes, was "the greatest tragedy since the Son of God died on a cross,"[8] Jones wrote a memoir of his relationship with Gandhi, a book which was first published in 1948. In this memoir Jones describes Gandhi's efforts in March of 1948 to repair both the physical and spiritual destruction caused by the Hindu riots against Moslems which followed Britain's grant of independence to India in 1947. The immediate cause of the riots was the partition of the South Asian subcontinent into India, which is predominantly Hindu, and Pakistan, which is predominantly Moslem. Gandhi urged his fellow Hindus to restore property they had stolen or destroyed and to confess and go to jail for crimes they had committed during the anti-Moslem riots. Jones' comment is that Gandhi "was preaching a corporate and individual repentance to his people."[9]

The Growing Movement for Reconciliation

In North America God is moving the hearts of many different denominations and groups of Christians toward repentance of their sins against other Christians and toward a true spiritual ecumenism. This movement is perhaps most successful in reuniting pentecostals and evangelicals. Clark Pinnock, a Canadian evangelical theologian writing in the early 1980s, recognized the spiritual starvation of the millions of "discouraged saints" in American and Canadian pews. These disheartened Christians are the very heart and soul of the charismatic renewal movement because they "are simply thirsting for more of" Christ's fullness and "for greater warmth from the spiritual fire within."[10] Addressing his evangelical colleagues, Pinnock says, "May we not be too proud or too fearful to recognize the testimony of our Pentecostal brethren, and add their dynamism to our doctrine."[11]

Perhaps the most widely known effort to unite evangelicals and pentecostals is the ministry of Texas evangelist James Robison. With the publication of his best-selling *Thank God I'm Free* in the mid-1980s Robison turned from his parochial and exclusive message to Southern Baptists and other traditional evangelical American Christians to embrace pentecostals and charismatics. "We have made idols," he wrote to his ministry partners in 1987, "of men, movements, ministries and denominations. The traditions of men have been exalted above the principles of God."[12] Robison accepted the pentecostal and charismatic rediscovery of the importance of the person and power of the Holy Spirit and was personally and professionally transformed as an explosively effective American evangelist and more recently, as a missionary evangelist to the war-ravaged in Mozambique, Bosnia and other distressed parts of the world. Writing to his partners and other Christians about the foolish and sinful divisiveness and partisanship within the American Church, Robison said, "I promise you that I will not accept division. I will seek to bring true, scriptural, spiritual oneness to the Body of Christ. my heart cries out for the healing of the Body. It must be healed. ... Instead of discussing the works of Jesus, let's do them."[13]

James Robison's ministry of restoration between evangelicals on the one hand and pentecostals and charismatics on the other is certainly close to the heart of God. But Robison's ministry is not close enough to the Kingdom of God, because it seeks to reconcile only one group of conservative American Christians with another group of conservative American Christians. In the past two decades several groups have been formed with the goal of effecting a unity within the American Church which is much broader than Robison's ministry of restoration. Ronald J. Sider's Evangelicals for Social Action and the People's Christian Coalition which publishes *Sojourners*, edited by Jim Wallis, are the two most prominent organizations which seek to bring the advocates of liberal social justice together with traditional evangelicals. However, no group has to date conceived of the Kingdom of God as the goal of the *whole* Body of Christ, the goal of the Church for which Christ died in order to "sanctify it" so that "he might present it to himself a glorious church, not having spot, or wrinkle, or any such thing." (Ephesians 5:25-26KJV).

In fact, no one has yet touched the depth of spiritual starvation among all of God's saints, from the most free-wheeling liberal to the most tradition-bound conservative, in the American Body of Christ. A Gallup poll conducted in June, 1984 for Robert H. Schuller Ministries asked questions of a nationwide sample of 1522 adults with respect to the issue of how Christian liberals and conservatives can be brought together in the United States. Sixty-eight percent (68%) of those responding to the survey thought "greater understanding between conservative and liberal Christians would be desirable." However, only 16% of the respondents "is actively involved in bringing about greater understanding among different groups of Christians."[14]

This deep longing of the American spirit for the reconciliation of Christian liberals and conservatives is in fact a profound yearning for repentance. God can only move through the power of His Holy Spirit to heal when we come naked, wounded and bleeding to Him, confessing our sins and pleading for forgiveness and reconciliation. God, of course, has already reconciled us to Himself, through His own brokenness in the death of His Son, our only Savior, Jesus the Christ. But American Christians cannot satisfy the yearning in the heart of God for restoration of religious liberals and conservatives until and unless we repent, both individually and collectively, and show that our hearts are prepared to forgive so that we may receive a fuller measure of God's grace.

In an earlier chapter on the past, present and future of the charismatic renewal movement, we traced the history of American evangelicalism from its nineteenth century origin to the time when it gave birth to the pentecostal and charismatic movements in the twentieth century. We emphasized that American evangelicals in the nineteenth century were intimately involved in social reform. Evangelicals were the key leaders of the abolition movement, the women's movement and the movement to improve the socio-economic condition of the urban working class and of the poor. In fact, without the leadership of evangelical Christians none of these movements would have succeeded in the United States.

We also suggested earlier why twentieth century American evangelicals, including pentecostals and charismatics, have lost their spiritual zeal for social, economic and political change. The roots of the contemporary bifurcation of American Christianity into liberals, who advocate institutional and collective salvation, and pentecostals and charismatics, who advocate individual salvation, lies in the catastrophic dilemma of slavery and of the racism which slavery produced. So, if pentecostals and charismatics are to be reunited with the advocates of liberal social justice, reconciliation must begin with the issue which first separated them.

Repentance must begin in the United States as it began with a single member of a United Methodist Church in Anderson, South Carolina when he wrote a letter to the editor of the *South Carolina United Methodist Advocate*, a weekly newspaper published by the South Carolina Conference of the United Methodist Church. His letter included these words: "I made a motion in the official body of the church to put in the local paper, to ask for forgiveness for our indifference and hypocrisy, and let it be known that all people were welcome at our church regardless of race."[15]

Three Parables of Repentance

Ultimately, Christian repentance is a mystery, a mystery which cannot be directly described. Repentance is best explained indirectly through the use of parables. The following three parables are based on our experience at Indianapolis 1990, the Congress on the Holy Spirit and World Evangelization held in Indianapolis in August, 1990 and sponsored by the North American Renewal Service Committee. Marcia was on the Local Steering Committee for the Congress. She wrote the following three parables.

I. The Parable of the Pink Dress

During the Congress my dear sister and her two friends from Spartanburg, South Carolina stayed with Boo and me in our small house with one bathroom. Suffice it to say, we all became rather close under compact conditions. Despite the demanding and wearing effects of the Congress, I was determined to let hospitality be my watchword. Trying too hard to be gracious sometimes sets the scene for a singular stupidity or a whole string of snaffus. Sister's friend and our new acquaintance Sandra and her pretty pink dress were props for one singular stupidity -- with my name written all over it.

To make the story short, I wash pretty pink dress in washing machine along with apt-to-run purple pants. Dress ruined. Sandra kept in dark about my blunder until I try Clorox II and Spray and Wash to no avail. Armed with copious apologies and a Martha of Bethany complex, I am hide-bound to fix things -- my way. That afternoon during lunch break, I finagle sister to help me shop for suitable replacement. Scanning rack after rack of women's wear proves to be wasted effort -- not so much because of limited selection but more because I'm going against the grain. God isn't in this self-imposed shopping search and deep down I sense it.

Sensitive to the Spirit, sister finally gently confronts my compulsion. We talk it out and I agree that I'm simply frustrating myself with an old lingering pattern to fix messes of my own making *my way*. My way is not *the* Way and won't work. In prayer and pondering, I receive the convicting grace of the Spirit and release from my worrisome sin.

Sandra was certainly more than understanding and forgiving. The old me didn't want to accept her forgiveness. But the Spirit freed me through parable, parable which instructed: "You persist in wanting to fix mistakes and wrongs which only I can fix. Stop it. Stop fretting. Be still and let me fix that which only I can fix." It was good to let go and get out of the compulsion trap. A Congress extra: a parable in a pink dress tailor-made just for me.

2. Hall C -- No Accident

In 1946 E. Stanley Jones' *The Way* was published. In it he talks about the naturalness of the Christian way. With an unself-conscious writing sytle that is pure anointing, my co-favorite Christian author (sharing this distinction with John Wesley) says, "The soul is unnaturally pagan. When it is pagan, it is off center, missing the way to live. When it becomes Christian, it has a sense of home-coming, of being reinstated, of being reconciled. The soul instinctively knows that this is the Way."[16] Jones stuffs two weeks' worth of powerful teaching into three words: *"realized in him."* (I John 2:8Moffatt). Elaborating on this text from John's gospel, he says, "We are realized in Him; we come to our own, become ourselves, are truly natural. It is simple, literal fact that the more I belong to Him, the more I belong to myself. The more I am bound to Him, the freer I am."[17]

I do not want to be sectarian for that is wrong. The Lord has not brought me *this* far in *the Walk* for me to wallow in sticky, divisive partisanship. I dare not pervert His outrageous grace by idolizing my denomination or indulge in mere sentimentality. I can only state the truth of what I know and felt. The moment I walked into Hall C on Thursday morning, I knew instinctively that I was "at home." In some special way which I don't fully understand, and in the penetrating way that E. Stanley Jones sums up the matter -- "To know God as revealed in Christ, in the sense of participating in, is life eternal. It is also life natural."[18] I am fulfilled, at home with, and truly natural among the people called Methodist. God had something just for me in Hall C. That I was there was no accident.

In his thundering book, *Run To The Battle*, Roberts Liardon speaks of two anointings. Super-charged truth nuggets are strategically set on each page and explode without warning like land mines in the reader's face. Chapter 8 speaks of the need for confrontation and change. Roberts Liardon says, "Confrontation can come in a variety of ways, ranging from a gentle hint to a bold word that hits hard. How it comes, when it comes, and through whom it comes should all be directed by the Holy Spirit."[19] Zeroing in on the need for confrontational change in the Body of Christ, Liardon discerns two anointings:

> There is a powerful sweet anointing and a powerful bold anointing. Both are from God, but if you only accept one of them, you will have a problem. If you stay stuck in the sweet, you will never know the bold.

> If you stay stuck in the bold, you will never know the sweet. You need to know how to flow back and forth between the two as the Spirit leads.[20]

The God-ordained "sweet anointing" prevailed in Hall C and invaded and pervaded my hungry spirit. It was reported that the Prayer Committee upon visiting hall C prior to the Congress' opening sensed a deep, strong, reverential, sweet spirit in this place. The same Spirit that enabled the disciples to "express themselves" as recorded in Acts 2:4(Moffatt) engulfed Hall C and me, enabling us all to be "so poised, so natural, so altogether alinve and spontaneous" -- and sweetly so. Jones describes this as "self-expression through Spirit-possession." I felt such warmth and kinship with all the folks in Hall C. We seemed most ourselves because we were most God's. I seemed, we all seemed entirely free from "inhibitions, fears, guilts" as the Spirit stirred us to be natural in worship, praise, prayer, giftings, fellowship so that we were truly "supernaturally natural" in the presence of God.[21]

Is it any wonder that in such an atmosphere of surrender that I received the beginning of release from rejection and a new degree of knowing that God's hand was upon me to perfect me in His divine destiny for my life? My healing deliverance from the long-buried fear of God's rejecting me began that Thursday morning in Hall C. A dear, sweet couple from Dr. Jimmy's church in Tulsa prayed for me and the Spirit poured His power to help me let go dreaded rejection, which I did not know hid deep within me, over my spirit and unburdened my wounded heart, softened it for a new work of revival, restoration and grace. It was *here* that I began to grasp the truth that the task I thought was mine -- the task of somehow amassing, covering and interpreting the Congress -- was off base. God was going to customize this Congress for me, personalize it and otherwise reveal to me that my perspective was not His perspective, that I was just embarking on a price paying plan that, in its initial stage, served to expose how ill prepared and out of position I was to do anything but focus on my shortcomings and changes required to overcome my own spiritual darkness and resistance to the Holy Spirit. Thank God for Hall C, the sweet anointing and the people called Methodist. At least it was a beginning.

3. The Parable of the Dancing Twins

The last night of the Congress when Boo, our three houseguests and I were sitting in one of the way far back side sections of the Hoosier Dome, God showed me how He expects us to treat offenses and stay free of the bondage of offendedness.

I was past tired. I was utterly exhausted. The children far down below us at floor level in the center back were not tired, not exhausted. They were God's true worshippers that night. In what can only be described as a trance-like state, I watched lively little ones join hands and dance a circle with abandon. Then it happened in a spectral split-second. One of a pair of twins got tangled in her own feet and landed hard on the hard floor. A smiling face framed by two long pony tails sticking out the side of her small head turned to a silent cry of pain. Up she sprang, smarting with agony turned to anger and shoved her sister as if to say, "Why'd you make me fall?" Her sister playfully pushed her as if to say, "Hey, come on! Snap out of it. We're dancing, remember?" In less than a heart beat, the offended sister taking her sister's hand burst into happiness and flung herself once more into the dance as if nothing at all had happened. To underscore the lightning speed with which the scene I've described took place, I didn't even have time to think, "Uh-oh, I wonder what will happen. Jesus, don't let this devil-fetched accident break up the harmony of the dance and don't let her be hurt from falling down." No, no. It all was so ultra quick. And the Inner Voice whispered, "This is how the Church must react to offenses. Dance and keep on dancing together in absolute childlike oblivion. Don't let go of each other's hands and don't refuse to re-take the hand of your sister when you fall down by accident, or circumstance or deliberate willfulness. Got it?"

Hallelujah! I got it. Holy Spirit, drive this lesson into my spirit and don't let me forget it. Never ever.

A Closer Look

The golden thread running through each of these overly personalized and admittedly esoteric and compacted "parables" is the need for repentance.

In the case of the first we see the sin of *pride* or the *fear* of being diminished, which produces the unreality born of refusal to relinquish my claim to myself.

In the case of the second, we detect the sin of *perversion* presiding to effect rejection which is rooted in the *fear* of self-surrender, of letting go one's secret self-loathing or of the supposed right to condemn one's self.

In the case of the third, we recognize the sin of *protracted hardness of heart* stemming from a triple threat: the *fear* of failure, *fear* of being misunderstood and *fear* of lacking self-worth, which almost always leads to offense-taking.

Wow. That's quite a mouthful. What a complicated diagnosis of psychoses, impossible to untangle. To mix the metaphor, and, in the attempt to simplify, let's boil it down to one single sin. *Fear* is its name. In this context an apt rendering of the well-coined refrain, "The need is the call.", might be, "The *need* to repent is the *call* to repent." And God says it is His goodness not human harshness which effects repentance. (See Romans 2:4). Moreover, for each side, conservative charismatic/pentecostal and liberal social justice proponents, not to name their fears, not to see the sinful disposition, the duplicity and complicity in pride, perversion, protracted hardness of heart *and* concomitant *fear* (of self, of God, of the other) is not only to clench the teeth, fold the arms of seething suspicion and turn away from each other and the call to repentance that would effect real renewal, it is also (and much more serious?) a refusal of that special tenderness of Love and Light which is the only Way out of the dark and back Home. The way out of the morass, the way back to reunification, restoration, renewal and release is always, "I will go to my Father and say..." In the words of George MacDonald, "Say to Him, 'My God, I am very dull and low and hard; but Thou art wise and high and tender, and Thou art my God [and my brother's God]. I am thy child. Forsake me not.'"[22]

Notes

1. Lovelace, p. 383.
2. *Ibid.*, p. 382.
3. Soeldner, p. 19.
4. Fowler, pp. 14-15.
5. Quebedeaux, 1978, p. 167.
6. Breckenridge, p. 31.
7. Archbishop Kirill, p. 266.
8. Jones, 1983, p. 11.
9. *Ibid.*, p. 14.

10. Pinnock, p. 16.
11. *Ibid.*
12. Robison, p. 4.
13. *Ibid.*, p. 8.
14. Princeton Religion Research Center, p. 2.
15. Deanhardt.
16. Jones, 1946, p. 32.
17. *Ibid.*, p. 41.
18. *Ibid.*
19. Liardon, p. 109.
20. *Ibid.*, p. 110.
21. Jones, 1946, p. 40.
22. Tileston, p. 162.

For Further Reading and Reflection

We began this chapter by using John the Baptist as the New Testament pattern for repentance and renewal. An insightful and anointed comparison of John the Baptist and Jesus Christ can be found in James S. Stewart, *The Life and Teaching of Jesus Christ* published by Abingdon (no date) pp. 35-38.

It is interesting to compare criticism between and among American Christians today with criticism among Christians in the eighteenth century. John Wesley admired and was influenced by the Moravians. When he was asked whether he thought that even the Moravian Church was "perfect, without spot, or wrinkle, or any such thing," he answered, "No; though I trust it will be, when patience has had its perfect work. But neither do I think it right to entertain the world with the spots of God's children." *The Works of John Wesley. Vol. l: Journal From October 14, 1735 to November 29, 1745.* Grand Rapids, Michigan: Zondervan, no date. For a discussion of the influence of Pietism on the Moravians and on John Wesley see (Brown).

Near the end of this chapter we discussed the growing movement for reconciliation and ecumenism between evangelicals and pentecostals and charismatics and between evangelicals and advocates of liberal social justice. The South African theologian Henry Lederle emphasizes the fact that genuine ecumenism is not a merger of ecclesiastical institutions nor a conference of churches seeking interfaith dialogue. True ecumenism is and must be "a spiritual matter." (Koenig and Lederle, p. 4).

The charismatic renewal movement according to one of its popular spokesmen "has introduced a grassroots kind of ecumenism to evangelicals that they had never known before." (Quebedeaux, 1978, p. 98). The New Zealand Anglican and leader of charismatic renewal in his church, D. H. Battley, says that the charismatic movement "is God's address to the Church in an age when faith is uncertain, the wounds of the believers are great, and the task is seemingly beyond us." *International Review of Mission*, vol. 75 (April 1986), p. 154.

If the charismatic renewal movement is to be truly ecumenical, based on an ecumenism of the Holy Spirit, and if it is in fact, "God's address" to His people, then like all authentic messages from God, it must begin with repentance and forgiveness.

The role of the Church in repentance and renewal extends beyond the Church itself. The political culture of every society must also be periodically renewed. Renewal

> is the product of Spirit-filled confessional situations. The Church performs an indispensable ministry to the political world by calling individuals and groups to confession and providing enduring contexts for it. Paul Valliere, *Holy War and Pentecostal Peace*. New York: Seabury, 1983, p. 143.

Donald W. Shriver, Jr., the President of Union Theological Seminary in New York City, has said that "the church's relation to the world is a rhythm of obedience, repentance and renewal." What Can Liberals and Evangelicals Teach Each Other? *The Christian Century*, vol. 104 (August 12-19, 1987) p. 689. In the United States today there is no greater spiritual need than the need for the church to lead the nation in confession of its corporate sins, in prayers of repentance and in calls for renewal.

In this chapter we discussed two organizations which united American evangelicals with advocates of liberal social justice -- Evangelicals for Social Action and the People's Christian Coalition. An even more comprehensive group is Renovare. Renovare was formed under the leadership of Richard J. Foster, a Quaker theologian and author of *Celebration of Discipline*. The organization combines five streams of Western Christianity: the contemplative or prayer-filled stream, the evangelical or word-centered stream, the holiness or virtuous life stream, the spirit-empowered or charismatic stream and the social justice or compassionate life stream. The Board of Reference of Renovare is a Who's Who of contemporary American Christianity including Jamie Buckingham (now deceased); Ted W. Engstrom, President Emeritus of World Vision; Millard Fuller, Founder of Habitat for Humanity; Martin Marty of the University of Chicago Divinity School; Henri J. M. Nouwen; C. Peter Wagner; Bishop Richard B. Wilke of the United Methodist Church and John Wimber.

Finally, for a report on an effort to unite charismatics and evangelical social activists, see Charismatics Shake Hands With Activists, *Christianity Today*, vol. 32 (February 19, 1988) p. 58; and for an account of a meeting between pentecostals and the National Council of Churches, see K. Houghland, Pentecostals and NCC Begin Dialogue, *The Christian Century*, vol. 104 (January 28, 1987) pp. 87-89.

Chapter 5

One in Mind and Spirit

> Christianity, at its biblical core, is neither a conservative nor a liberal option. It is downright radical. "Love your enemies." How radical can you get? Christ demands that his followers take up their cross and travel a narrow way that can never be popular. In many ways that demand challenges almost all the values of the wider culture that Christians often take up as a *compromise* because the way of the cross is just too hard.
>
> -- Richard Quebedeaux

American pentecostalism was born at 312 Azusa Street in Los Angeles, California in April 1906. The Holy Spirit was so powerfully present at the Azusa Street Mission that, according to Frank Bartleman, an eyewitness, participant and later a leader in the American pentecostal movement, when "men came within two or three blocks of the place, they were seized with conviction."[1] Because those who came to Azusa Street sought God so earnestly and submitted themselves so completely to the direction of the Holy Spirit, the meetings were altogether under God's control. There were no designated meeting times, no order of worship and no formal leadership. "All was spontaneous, ordered by the Spirit."[2] And when the Spirit moved upon the congregation, "God Himself would give the altar call. Men would fall all over the house, like the slain in battle, or rush for the altar en masse to seek God. The scene often resembled a forest of fallen trees. Such a scene cannot be imitated. I never saw an altar call given in those early days. God Himself would call them."[3]

Moreover, the authenticity of the fresh anointing of the Holy Spirit at the dilapidated mission on Azusa Street in Los Angeles in 1906 was confirmed by the subsequent creation and growth of pentecostal churches and denominations in the United States and throughout the world. The story of this phenomenal growth of the pentecostal movement is well known. What is often ignored or forgotten, however, is the fact that the Azusa Street Revival was led by an American black man, William J. Seymour. For Seymour himself, the mid-wife of the rebirth of the Holy Spirit in the twentieth century, who lived at a time when racism was at its worst in the United States, when Jim Crow laws made racial prejudice official in the South and unofficial custom and practice made racial hate the unquestioned rule of public opinion in the rest of the nation, the pentecost he experienced at Azusa Street was not merely a personal revelation of God's grace. Pentecost for Seymour during the Azusa Street revival "meant to love in the face of hate, to overcome the hatred of a whole nation" and to establish himself as a legitimate Christian leader among people who were spiritually imprisoned by their racial intolerance.[4] In a very real sense the "'color line' was washed away in the blood" of Jesus Christ.[5]

The Neglect of Corporate Salvation

Ignoring the racial roots of American pentecostalism symbolizes the larger neglect of the social, economic and political aspects of human life by both pentecostals and charismatics for nearly 100 years. The pentecostal theologian Gerald T. Sheppard, commenting on the contemporary American charismatic renewal movment, notes that the "ecumenism of the Spirit" which came out of charismatic renewal cound have provided a bridge back to the roots of pentecostalism in the black church and in Hispanic pentecostalism. Sheppard says, "If that bridge had been bravely and humbly crossed, charismatic renewal could have wedded the moral, economic, and political fruits of the Holy Spirit more securely to the flamboyant public exercise of the charismata."[6] Instead, American pentecostals and charismatics have focused almost exclusively on the personal salvation of individual souls, have identified themselves with the social, economic and political status quo and have missed the radically comprehensive command of God to proclaim the Gospel to institutions and structures as well as to individuals.

The Holy Spirit does not bring the conviction of sin to spiritually isolated persons nor do such sinners under conviction repent and receive forgiveness and salvation by themselves. According to Dale W. Brown, who has researched the relationship between Pietism and evangelicalism, we "do not become converted and then join others who have had similar experiences; rather, relationships with others are a part of God's converting action."[7] The integral role of the community of faith in doing the work of the Kingdom of God on earth means that evangelical Christians, including pentecostal and charismatic Christians, must expand their definition of the gifts of the Holy Spirit so that the use of the gifts of wisdom, knowledge, discernment and prophecy, for example, will expose not just personal sins like abortion and homosexuality but also economic and political sins like the greed and human exploitation of American business corporations and the moral cowardice of elected and appointed government officials who slavishly follow public opinion (instead of leading it) by subsidizing the toabcco industry and by eagerly financing and glorifying the human carnage of the Persian Gulf War.

In 1986 the *International Review of Mission*, recognizing the person and power of the Holy Spirit in the charismatic renewal movement as the key to the mission and evangelistic outreach of the Church, devoted several of its monthly issues exclusively to charismatic renewal throughout the world. Eugene L. Stockwell, the editor of *IRM*, stated in an editorial in one of these issues that the desperate struggles of Chinese Christians against religious and political persecution, of men and women in many two-thirds world nations to secure human rights from repressive military dictatorships, of Africans against racism, of Christians in the United States and in the [former] Soviet Union against militarism and of Christians everywhere to end world hunger are all "surely charismatic."[8]

Cardinal Leon Joseph Suenens, a sympathetic observer of the international charismatic renewal movement in the Catholic Church, has said that a true Christian is both charismatic and socially committed. There is no genuine Christian who is not charismatic and socially committed.[9]

This international recognition of the corporate and institutional character of the charismatic renewal movement is reflected in the acknowledgment by the American pentecostal leader Murray W. Dempster that "social justice ... should be modelled within the pentecostal community as a social witness to the power of the

Gospel."[10]

Having documented in this and previous chapters the urgent and persistend need of the Holy Spirit for Christians who preach and practice the *whole* Gospel, including the good news of the Kingdom of God for both individuals and socio-economic and political institutions, the question remains, how can Christians fulfill this deepest need in the heart of God for *one* Church united within itself because it is united to Him? In the remainder of this chapter we will use the New Testament to demonstrate how truly radical the command of the Gospel is.

The New Testament Church

The "truly Pentecostal Church," according to one observer, "needs to return to a holistic view of the gospel as visibly practiced and proclaimed by the first century Church."[11] This wholistic view of the Gospel begins with the faith of the writers of the New Testament in the redemptive power of the resurrected Christ and in the continuing presence of the Holy Spirit. Their faith was a "shining, blazing certainty," not the "tentative and uncertain faith" which is characteristic of many contemporary Christian churches.[12] In the first century church there was no accumulated body of theological doctrine, no ecclesiastical hierarchy and no long tradition of worship and liturgy to restrain the flow of the Holy Spirit. J. B. Phillips, the outstanding sholar and translator of the Bible, comments that the "fresh air of Heaven blows gustily through" the pages of the New Testament and that even "ordinary human life" described by the writers of the New Testament "is continually open to the Spirit of God."[13]

Although Phillips wrote about the New Testament church in the 1950s, his description of the spiritual malaise of Christianity and of the need for a new outpouring of the love of God applies to the church in the 1990s and beyond just as much as it applied to the church 40 years ago. We need a fresh anointing from the Holy Spirit today because we are all twentieth century Americans conditioned by "the mental climate of our age" to regard our lives as a "completely closed system of cause and effect."[14] In the face of this mental climate, Phillips said, a fresh anointing "can only come from God Himself" and "it can only be received by those who are willing to be open to God and ready to cooperate with His purpose."[15]

In the years since Phillips wrote about the need for a new outpouring of and a new receptivity to God's love, the charismatic renewal movement has responded to that need. But the charismatic renewal has not completely fulfilled the need for God's love because it has not yet presented the whole Gospel, the Gospel which includes the Good News of corporate and institutional as well as personal salvation. In the words of Cardinal Leon Joseph Suenens, who closely monitors the Catholic charismatic renewal, and of Dom Helder Camara, a leader in the movement for social justice in Latin America, "*All* the commandments and the *entire* gospel must be incorporated into the *whole* of life."[16]

The whole Gospel is the Gospel which transforms both persons and institutions, the Gospel which speaks to individuals in the context of their families, their possessions and their relationships to other ethnic and religious groups. The first century church described by Luke in the book of Acts was a community of individuals transformed by the Holy Spirit with respect to each of these aspects of human life. When Peter preached to the crowd in Jerusalem in Acts 2, he quoted from Joel's Old Testament prophesy that in the last days God would pour out His Spirit on all flesh, both men and women without regard to sex. And in Acts 2:44-45 as well as in Acts 4 and 5 Luke describes how the believers in the early church shared their possessions with each other according to individual needs. Later, in Acts 10 Peter's vision of the ritually clean and unclean animals overcame ethnic differences between Jews and Gentitles. Finally, Acts 19 records the end of religious distinctions within the community of believers when the followers of John the Baptist were baptized and received the Holy Spirit so that the disciples of John were united with the disciples of Jesus.[17]

The Christian church as portrayed by Luke in the book of Acts practiced what we would today call "culturally sensitive evangelism."[18] According to John Amstutz "[a]lthough the door into the household of faith was low, low enough to require all men to bow in humble repentance and faith in God's gift, it was wide enough that men of any nation could enter without losing their cultural identity."[19] In one of the last books he wrote before his death, E. Stanley Jones says that the New Testament model for the contemporary church should not be the church at Jerusalem (as described in Acts), which was based on hierarchy and racial exclusiveness, but the church at Antioch, which was founded by laymen on the principles of democracy and inclusiveness.[20]

The Revolutionary Church

Because it was culturally sensitive, because it treated men and women as truly equal partners in the work of the Kingdom of God on earth and because it abolished and transcended the most immediate and most dangerous threat to the Christian community -- the difference between Jews and Gentiles -- the New Testament church was truly radical. In fact, the church was revolutionary. John H. Yoder, the intellectually brilliant and spiritually gifted Mennonite theologian and social and political ethicist, suggests that we should translate the Greek word *euangelion*, from which we derive our words "evangel" and "evangelism," as "revolution" instead of as "good news." Yoder says that *euangelion* means not just another "welcome piece of information" but profound truth "which impinges upon the fate of the community."[21]

Sociologists Luther P. Gerlach and Virginia H. Hine also use the term "revolutionary" to describe the gospel message of salvation in their comparison of the Black Power movement and American pentecostalism. American pentecostalism in the early twentieth century, like the first century Christian church, confronted "both unbelievers and nominal Christians with the fact of a transforming experience," an experience which revolutionized not only the personal relationship of individual converts to God but also their corporate relationship to their families, their churches and to their culture and society.[22]

The kind of revolution proclaimed by Jesus Christ was not the extirpation of the Roman Empire from Palestine as Jesus' disciples assumed. The revolution proclaimed by Jesus was the revolution of the Kingdom of God, a revolution which was much more radical than any political or military revolution because it transformed not just socio-economic institutions and governments; Jesus' revolution transformed the hearts of men; it changed "human nature."[23]

Revolutionary Subordination

At the heart of the revolution of Jesus Christ is the reality of "revolutionary subordination." The Kingdom of God announced by Jesus is not merely an "alternative to present experience but rather a renewed way of living within the present."[24] This is what Jesus meant when he prayed for his disciples in John 17, asking God not to take them out of the world, but ... to keep them safe from the Evil One." (John 17:15TEV). Paul does not urge slaves to revolt against their masters nor does he suggest that masters enslave themselves in order to identify and empathize with slaves. Instead, Paul like Jesus preaches revolutionary subordination. The subordinate Christian freely accepts his or her status as an act of revolutionary subordination. On the other hand, the socially, economically or politically superior Christian must not use his power or status to dominate or exploit his subordinates.[25]

The revolution of the Kingdom of God is not a violent revolution. It is a revolution which is much more radical than any political or military revolution, no matter how bloody. The revolution of the Kingdom of God is a revolution begun with Jesus' resurrection and consummated at Pentecost. Yoder states, "Since in the resurrection and in Pentecost the kingdom which was imminent has now in part come into our history, the church can now live out, within the structures of society, the newness of the life of that kingdom.[26]

Can a Good End Justify Evil Means?

Just how radical is the Kingdom of God? No principle of Christian social ethics is more cherished than the principle of the relationship between means and ends. And no moral question has been more thoroughly and heatedly debated throughout the history of the church than the question of whether a good end justifies evil means. For the Christian who truly accepts the revolution of the Kingdom of God, however, there is *no* morally justifiable relationship between evil means and good ends. Every human act must be judged by the same radical Kingdom criterion. No evil, however small in comparison to some greater good, or however necessary to produce a greater good, can be justified in the Kingdom of God. The crucial question is whether Jesus is Lord. If He is Lord, then He is the only standard of legitimacy; He is in control of history and questions of means and ends are irrelevant.[27]

Ultimately, the principle of revolutionary subordination is the principle of subordinating oneself as well as one's family, one's business, one's school, one's church and one's government to the Kingdom of God. There is no better example of this principle of revolutionary subordination and of the principle of the moral independence of means and ends than E. Stanley Jones' attitude toward war.

> If war is right, Christ is wrong; and if Christ is right, war is wrong. If Christ stays in this world, war must go. If war stays, Christ must go. Or if He does stay, He must be blown to pieces on a thousand battlefields.
>
> Christ and war are irreconcilables. They are not "compossible." If I must make my choice, I choose Him. Therefore I renounce war.[28]

Jesus' command to love not only our neighbor but our enemy also rests on these same principles of revolutionary subordination and of judging the morality of all human action strictly on its own merits without regard to its causes or its results. This is why war is always wrong. In order to fight, man must hate and hatred of other human beings, according to the New Testament, is always wrong. But the Gospel of Jesus Christ is not just the ethical prohibition, do not hate your brother and sister. The Good News [of the Kingdom] empowers us to replace, to overrule hate with love, for when we truly love God, as Jesus Himself demonstrated on the cross, then we no longer want to hate and "the love of God is shed abroad in our hearts by the Holy Ghost." (Romans 5:5KJV). And we love others, even our enemies, not "because Jesus told us to. We love our neighbor because God is like that."[29] Through Jesus' death and resurrection and through the coming of the Holy Spirit at Pentecost God is calling us to be like Himself. This is the only standard the New Testament gives us to evaluate the morality of any human behavior, whether it is individual or corporate behavior. The question to raise is "Is the behavior what God would Himself sanction or do?"

Politics and Government in the New Testament

Jesus' ethical commandment to do what God would do is especially relevant to politics and government. The New Testament gospels contain almost no direct references to God's moral requirements for political behavior. Paul's letters and the second chapter of I Peter, however, offer instruction about the individual Christian's obligation to political authority and about the obligation of the church to pray for government. In I Timothy 2:2TEV Paul urges Timothy to have the church pray "for kings and all others who are in authority, that we may live a quiet and peaceful life with all reverence toward God and with proper conduct."

Paul is certainly saying that the proper function of government is to maintain peace and order among the citizens who are subject to its authority. But more important, Paul is describing the role and status of Christian believers in a community consisting of both believers and nonbelievers. Christian personal and political conduct must be morally unquestionable, Paul writes, because "God our Savior ... wants everyone to be saved and to come to know the truth." (I Timothy 2:3-4TEV). In other words, Christians should not grieve the Holy Spirit by disobeying government officials or by disobeying God's law of love in any other way. For the sake of the Kingdom of God Christians must as nearly as possible on earth, exemplify moral perfection -- Christlikeness -- in all their actions and relationships. God is love. The Kingdom way is the way of love. As E. Stanely Jones was fond of saying, you don't have to love your fellow human beings; but if you choose not to love others as Christ commanded, you won't get along with them.

I Peter 2:13-17 contains ethical admonitions about the political responsibility of Christian citizenship which are similar to Paul's advice to Timothy in I Timothy 2. Peter tells his readers to obey the Roman Emperor and the Roman governors "for the sake of the Lord" because "God wants you to silence the ignorant talk of foolish people by the good things you do." (I Timothy 2:13, 15TEV).

For twentieth century Americans Romans 13:1-7 seems to present a moral standard of political conduct that is different from the standard established in I Timothy 2 and I Peter 2. Political officials, Paul writes to the Romans, derive their authority from God Himself. Christians must be politically obedient and pay both their personal and property taxes, because God has created governments and given their officers legitimate authority over other citizens.

To citizens of a nation founded on a successful challenge to the political and military authority of Great Britain in the late eighteenth century, Paul's instruction to the Romans in Romans 13 sounds like a sweeping mandate for Christians to obey unconditionally and indiscriminately all goverment laws, rules and regulations, regardless of the moral character of the government which made the laws, rules and regulations. However, reading Romans 13:1-7 in the context of what precedes and follows these verses reveals Paul's real intention. The life which Paul is calling the Romans to lead is a life of revolutionary subordination: "be not conformed to this world: but be ye transformed by the renewing of your mind, that ye may prove what is that good, and acceptable, and perfect, will of God." (Romans 12:2KJV). Although God clearly authorizes government officials to use the power He has given them to preserve the peace and order of the communities for which they are responsible, the ultimate authority for the Christian believer is not embodied in any kingdom established by man. Sovereign power resides only in the Kingdom of God.

After all, the thrust of the Lord's verdict in response to the question about taxes to the emperor foils the slightest presumptuous usurpation. In ironic inverted order, Jesus established unequivocally the proper Kingdom relationship which requires a rendering unto God -- *first*! If anything is left over, then Caesar is welcome to it. Comparing scripture with scripture, this interpretation does not violate the command to "seek ye first the kingdom of God ..." (Matthew 6:33KJV). On the contrary it embraces, reinforces and advances the absoluteness of this command.

Reading Romans 13:1-7 as a statement of the ultimate authority of the Kingdom of God is confirmed by the verse which immediately follows this passage, Romans 13:8TEV: "Be under obligation to no one -- the only obligation you have is to love one another." And the obligation to love one another comes not from any earthly government but from God Himself, for whom all other obligations and allegiances are subordinate to the supreme loyalty to the one truly totalitarian order, namely, the Kingdom of God.

Paul's real meaning in Romans 13:1-7 is also disclosed by Romans 6:15TEV: "What, then? Shall we sin, because we are not under law but under God's grace?" In Romans 13 Paul is warning new Christians who are still experiencing the exhilaration of their freedom in Christ not to permit their liberty to become license. Freedom from the law of the Old Testament does not mean freedom from the demands of personal and political morality. Being free in Christ means freely accepting all these demands through the only power which makes it possible for us to be both citizens of an earthly kingdom and citizens of the Kingdom of God, namely, the power of Jesus Christ and of God's Holy Spirit. Our freedom in Christ rests on our faith in Christ, our faith in the ultimate eschatological triumph of His Kingdom as well as our faith in the immediate, earthly triumph of the ethics of revolutionary subordination. Although we are not marching to Zion as a result of our own efforts, Zion, in Yoder's words, "is still where we are going. We are marching to Zion because, when God lets down from heaven the new Jerusalem prepared for us, we want to be the kind of persons and the kind of community that will not feel strange there."[30]

The Kingdom of God Today

Is it possible in today's world with its unimaginable evils of genocide, torture, mass starvation and global poverty for us to live under the regime of revolutionary subordination in the Kingdom of God? One twentieth century American saint and prophet not only created a community based on the ethic of revolutionary subordination, he led an entire nation to confess its collective sin of racism and to repent by restoring justice to millions of United States citizens who had been the tragic victims of unspeakable cruelty for over 200 years. In the late 1950s this great American wrote, "Any religion that professes to be concerned about the souls of men and is not concerned about the slums that damn them, the economic conditions that strangle them and the social conditions that cripple them is a spiritually moribund religion awaiting burial."[31]

Martin Luther King, Jr. could rebuke the Church with these sharp words because he was himself a Baptist preacher and like all the best preachers, he preached his sermons first of all to himself. But King was not just a great preacher. He was a great American and a great spokesman for Christ's message of revolutionary subordination in the Kingdom of God. King's stature rests not only on his achievements within the American Church but also on his ability to touch the conscience of the entire nation when its elected representatives in Washington, D. C. passed what many consider to be the most important piece of legislation of the twentieth century -- the Civil Rights Act of 1964.

Martin Luther King's philosophy of nonviolent direct action, which was responsible for the moral and political success of the civil rights movement in the United States, worked because it was based on the Kingdom principle of revolutionary subordination. Although he probably would not have described himself as a charismatic Christian who extended the gospel message of personal salvation to the corporate salvation available under the auspices of the ethic of revolutionary subordination in the Kingdom of God, King in fact in his own life and through the American civil rights movement achieved the synthesis of personal piety and social justice which the church today so desperately needs.

In an earlier chapter of this book we identified the Protestant evangelical roots of social reform in the United States and traced these roots to their origin in the abolition movement in the early nineteenth century. Timothy Smith's classic history of the evangelical origin of American socio-economic and political reform during the 1800s quotes William Hosmer, a radical holiness Methodist and a leader of the anti-slavery movement: "Wicked laws not only may be broken, but absolutely must be broken; there is no other way to escape the wrath of God."[32] It is this sense of the radically absolute character of the Kingdom of God which the American Church needs today. Nothing but a genuinely totalitarian commitment to Jesus Christ and to His Gospel can restore the presence and power of the Holy Spirit to our individual and personal lives, to our families, to our business corporations, to our social organizations, to our national collective life and to our governments.

Notes

1. Bartleman, p. 52.
2. *Ibid.*, p. 59.
3. *Ibid.*, p. 61.
4. Hollenweger, p. 5.
5. Bartleman, p. 53.
6. Quoted in Quebedeaux, 1983, p. 239.
7. Brown, p. 145.
8. Stockwell, p. 114.
9. Suenens, p. 71.
10. Dempster, 1987, p. 137.
11. Amstutz, p. 212.
12. Phillips, p. 2.
13. *Ibid.*, pp. 8-9.
14. Phillips, p. 24.
15. *Ibid.*, p. 75.
16. Suenens and Camara, p. 34.
17. Dempster, 1987, p. 148.
18. Amstutz, p. 218.
19. *Ibid.*, p. 220.
20. Jones, 1970.
21. Yoder, 1977, p. 15.
22. Gerlach and Hine, p. xviii.

23. Phillips, p. 8.
24. Yoder, 1972, p. 190.
25. *Ibid.*
26. *Ibid.*, p. 192.
27. *Ibid.*, pp. 243-244.
28. Jones, 1936, p. 161.
29. Yoder, 1977, p. 51.
30. *Ibid.*, p. 159.
31. Washington, p. 38.

For Further Reading and Reflection

The charismatic movement "has long been labeled as a movement in search of a theology." In Search of a Charismatic Theology. *Christianity Today*, vol. 30 (May 16, 1986) p. 44. Other commentators echo this need for a charismatic theology. D. H. Battley, the New Zealand Anglican charismatic leader whom we have mentioned in earlier chapters, writes about the need for "painstaking theological engagement" within the charismatic renewal movement. Charismatic Renewal: A View From Inside. *The Ecumenical Review*, vol. 38 (January, 1986) p. 52.

An early and very impressive effort to write a full length pentecostal Biblical theology is Frederick Dale Bruner, *A Theology of the Holy Spirit: The Pentecostal Experience and the New Testament Witness.* Grand Rapids, Michigan: Eerdmans, 1970. For a post-liberal theology based on a rediscovery of the authority and primacy of Scripture, see Albert C. Outler, Toward a Postliberal Hermeneutics. *Theology Today*, vol. 42 (October, 1985) pp. 281-291. Moreover, George W. Harper, Renewal and Causality: Some Thoughts On A Conceptual Framework For A Charismatic Theology, *Journal of Ecumenical Studies*, vol. 24 (Winter, 1987) pp. 93-103; suggests that charismatic theology does not have to be based on God's extraordinary interventions in time and nature. Charismatic theology, according to Harper, should be fully consistent with the ordinary operation of natural law.

Finally, with respect to the concept of salvation, an interesting but unconvincing comparison of pentecostal and liberation theology is Miroslav Volf, Materiality of Salvation: An Investigation in the Soteriologies of Liberation and Pentecostal Theologies. *Journal of Ecumenical Studies*, vol. 26 (Summer, 1989) pp. 447-467. A more persuasive article on salvation is Ronald J. Sider and James Parker III, How Broad Is Salvation in Scripture? *In Word and Deed: Evangelism and Social Responsibility*, ed. Bruce Nicholls. Grand Rapids, Michigan: Eerdmans,

1986. Sider and Parker say that in the Old Testament salvation is social and corporate as well as personal but that salvation is always in the context of God's covenant relationship with Israel. In the New Testament salvation is also corporate but it appears within the context of the community of believers.

Although in this chapter we have not developed a theology for the charismatic renewal movement, we do suggest how a truly radical understanding of the New Testament is necessary for a charismatic theology which applies to social, economic and political dimensions and institutions as well as to individuals. Throughout the history of the Christian Church the problem with theology has been its divisiveness. The direct and immediate experience of believers with Jesus Christ and with God's Holy Spirit is first expressed in terms of beliefs and principles. These spiritual beliefs and principles become, in turn, doctrines and dogmas of the Church. Finally, established doctrines and dogmas become the raw material for Biblical and systematic theology. Christian beliefs, doctrines and theologies are not themselves divisive. Rather, it is sinful, insecure and fearful Christians who identify themselves with these beliefs, doctrines and theologies and become suspicious and paranoid about other Christians with somewhat different beliefs, doctrines and theologies who are the source of division. The result, which is only too well documented in the history of the Reformation, the Counter Reformation, the Inquisition and the interminable religious wars of European Christians, is intolerance, bigotry, prejudice and hatred. And, as Oswald Chambers would, doubtless with heavy heart, remind us, God is most definitely not on the side of our prejudices -- any of them!

How can this warfare based on theological differences be avoided? Two political scientists, H. Mark Roelofs and Glenn Tinder, answer this question in essentially the same way. Roelofs says that "the only way" to prevent tyranny and intolerable inequality in communities of fallible and corruptible persons is to establish as an absolute principle "the incommensurable value of personhood." (Roelofs, p. 562). Tinder says that "the idea of the exalted individual is the spiritual center of Western politics." Tinder, Can We Be Good Without God? *The Atlantic Monthly*, vol. 264 (December, 1989) p. 76. (Tinder's article is an excerpt from his book *The Political Meaning of Christianity* published by Louisiana State University Press). The problem with these ideas is that individualism, whether expressed in the form of the incommensurable value of personhood or of the concept of the exalted individual, can never truly protect individuals from corporate evil. In one of his earliest books, E. Stanley Jones writes: "We must call men not to loyalty to a belief but loyalty to a Person. We may be loyal to a belief and be dead spiritually, but we cannot be loyal to this Person and be other than alive spiritually. He creates belief.

He is the great Believer himself, and in the light of his radiant faith we cannot but believe. But we do not get Jesus from our beliefs, we get our beliefs from Jesus. And they must of necessity be under constant correction by his mind and Spirit." (Jones, 1925, pp. 174-175).

In this chapter we have presented the good news of the New Testament in terms of both a personal and also a collective socio-econimic and political ethic. The political aspects of the New Testament gospel are too often overlooked. Richard Bauckham says we should never forget that Jesus "died a victim of a political system." *The Bible in Politics: How to Read the Bible Politically*. Louisville, Kentucky: Westminster/John Knox, 1989, p. 149. In a similar vein, Jurgen W. Liias, an Episcopal rector in Massachusetts who is both a Christian pacifist and a charismatic Christian, uses the political meaning of Jesus' crucifixion to emphasize how utterly impotent military power has become since His resurrection. Chaismatic Power or Military Power? *The Christian Century*, vol. 100 (November 30, 1983) pp. 1110-1113.

Christians in the two-thirds world are usually more concerned about the socio-economic and political aspects of the gospel than are Christians in Western Europe and North America. One example of this institutional and corporate concern is an article on church renewal by Sumio Takatsu, the Anglican Bishop of South Central Brazil: Renewal and the Transfornation of Society. *Open to the Spirit: Anglicans and the Experience of Renewal*. London: Church House Publishing, 1987, pp. 90-103.

Like Christians from the two-thirds world European charismatics and pentecostals are also generally more sensitive to social, economic and political injustice than most American charismatics and pentecostals. See Murray W. Dempster, Pentecostal and Charismatic Scholars Call for End to Apartheid, which was reprinted from the Sixth Conference of Pentecostal and Charismatic Research in Europe in *Transaction: An International Evangelical Dialogue on Mission and Ethics*, vol. 9 (January-March, 1992) pp. 32-33.

Paul Sigmund, a political scientist who specializes in political philosophy, writes that the "New Testament attitude toward politics is an ambivalent one -- part of a larger ambivalence toward 'this world.'" Paul Sigmund, Christianity, Ideology, and Political Philosophy. *Essays on Christianity and Political Philosophy*, ed. George W. Carey and James V. Schall. Lanham, Maryland: University Press of America, 1984, p. 80. Another political scientist, Kenneth D. Wald, says that is is "foolhardy to assert that religious faith necessarily upholds democratic values." *Religion and Politics in the United States*. New York: St. Martin's, 1987, p. 285. Religion may either support or subvert democratic values. "The source of the paradox," according to Wald, "is simply that religious values are ambiguous with regard to politics." P. 284.

It is both false and deceptive to say that the American versions of representative democracy or of capitalism are more Christian than a totalitarian dictatorship or Marxist communism. *All* political and economic systems are relative to the Kingdom of God.

In this chapter we have considered both the political and the ethical dimensions of a Christian faith which incorporates personal as well as corporate salvation. This discourse could have been amplified by considering as well the Biblically-derived contention that there are those things in society that "cause" persons to sin. It is lamentable that in many ways the more avowedly Word-centered, vibrant and energizing party, whom we refer to as the conservative charismatic/pentecostal wing, have entirely overlooked those impersonal and sturctural causes of sin in our society. Jesus says clearly and distinctly in the gospels that His Kingdom confronts not only individuals in their private and personal lives but also the impersonal social order with the good news of removal of sin and sins and the cleansing and coordinating of the two in every area of relationship and every portion of their beings. According to Jesus, when the Son of Man comes his job will be to remove from his kingdom all those who work unrighteousness and all causes (impersonal) of unrighteousness. See Matthew 13:41Moffatt. But such amplification would draw us beyond the bounds of this chapter. For a more thorough examination of this teaching see E. Stanley Jones' *Victorious Living.*

Richard J. Mouw, the evangelical theologian and Christian social ethicist whom we used as a source earlier in this book, has also explored "how the link between life in the Spirit and the quest for structural justice might be sustained in a healthy manner." Life in the Spirit in an Unjust World. *Pneuma*, vol. 9 (Fall, 1987) p. 117. In this article Mouw asks, "Is it legitimate to identify the cries of revolutionary movements in South Africa with the promptings of the Spirit? Can we hear the recognizable voice of the Spirit in feminist calls for an end to patriarchal oppression...?" P. 121. Unfortunately, Mouw fails to answer these questions with a resounding Yes! On the other hand, however, he does point to the need for the advocates of liberal social justice to be more completely filled with the Holy Spirit. "The community of Christian activists desperately needs a revival of orthopathy, a seeking of the personal presence of the Holy Spirit." P. 127.

Chapter 6

The Kingdom of God Recovered

The Kingdom Is Life

Now we come to the heart of the matter. Our earlier assertion to make the Kingdom of God hermeneutic and dynamic for effecting reunification of our two opposing groups cannot fail to tickle the triune funnybone! Of course, it is beyond preposterous pretention to project the Kingdom of God in mere utilitarian fashion as primary instrument for even such a lofty purpose as reharmonizing discordant movements of the faith. But it has to be done. We have no recourse but to try "to project," "to utilize," "to fixate on," or "to be constrained by" -- take your pick -- the concept of the Kingdom of God because nothing else suffices.

In the first place, only the Kingdom is vast, undefinable and defining enough, radical, redemptive and refining enough, transforming, enlivening and powerful enough to "serve" as Master Program, as it were, for the task at hand. In the second place, the Kingdom is key to everything else there is; it is the answer to the whole of life because Jesus Christ made it so. Obviously, the Kingdom is more than Key or Answer to life. It is *Life*: *Life* revealed, enunciated, lived out incarnationally -- in the Life of the Word-Become-Flesh;[1] *Life* offered and obtained (because it is Gift) in "the kingdom of his dear Son." (Colossians l:13TEV).

More. "In Him we live and move and have our being." (Acts 17:28TRBVIME). *Moreover*. In Him (the Son) who has "the full nature of God" (Colossians l:19TEV and Colossians 2:9KJV) and in union with whom "all things 'consist' [KJV] or have their proper place" (Colossians 1:17TEV) the Master Plan, the Kingdom of God is disclosed, thereby disclosing Life; unfolded, thereby unfolding *Life* and simultaneously infolding all that rightly "fits" into it. *Most.* "...the government shall be upon His shoulder; and His name shall be called Wonderful, Counsellor, Mighty God, Everlasting Father, Prince of Peace. There shall be no end to the increase of His government or to the peace upon the throne of David and upon His kingdom, in that it is firmly established and supported in justice and righteousness from now on and for ever. The zeal of the Lord of hosts shall do this." (Isaiah 9:6-7TRBVIME). *Bottomline.* All lesser things -- including this identifiable division between the conservative pentecostal/charismatic and the liberal social justice branches -- is subordinate to and must finally surrender to the Ultimate, to that which is *Life*, to the Kingdom of God.

E. Stanley Jones and the Kingdom of God

What an enormous, unpayable debt we owe to E. Stanley Jones! As he unselfconsciously niched himself into history as the greatest internationally acclaimed missionary-evangelist ever to grace the planet, he became for his day, for ours and conceivably for all time to come the incomparable interpreter of the Kingdom of God.[2]

Some bright, anonymous admirer of the world-famous Christian leader has correctly observed that when Stanely Jones "found" the obfuscated version of the Kingdom of God to be "'largely inward and mystical or futuristic in heaven,'" he did not leave it thus. Rather, through his prolific writings, including his popular daily devotional volumes, he recoverd the emphasis of the Kingdom as "central in his evangelism" and "'...put it into life as *the* issue *now* [my emphasis], supplanting all the alternatives of communism, fascism and whatnot.'"[3]

Lest the significance of a lifetime's devoted energies to single-handed rescue, recovery and consequent centralizing of the Kingdom of God in his evangelism and teaching ministry be understated, we should hasten to let Stanley Jones speak for himself:

> But this Kingdom of God grips me, I am obsessed with it and I'll tell you why. First of all, Jesus was obsessed with it. It is safe to catch His obsessions. He was never wrong, never misled by a subordinate issue, never once entangled in the marginal and irrelevant. He made

> this Kingdom central. It was that around which everything else revolved. It was the central idea which gave coherence and meaning to all his other ideas.[4]

If Stanley Jones wrote it, we can safely assume its accuracy. Admitting parallel accounts, "the Kingdom of God" is a phrase Jesus used 100 times; "the church" only twice, "and both times in only one Gospel."[5] In succinct wording we have emphasis-plus to further galvanize and justify Stanley Jones' obstinate grip on the Kingdom of God, or rather, its tight grip on him.

The Legacy of E. Stanley Jones

Stanley Jones never considered himself a professional writer.[6] He wrote out of "an inner urge"[7] to meet a perceived need.

> I have not written for the sake of writing, or for the sake of material gain. Rather, I have seen a need and have tried to meet that need. Each book [And there have been nearly thirty titles.] has been aimed at some particular end. Having written for that specific need, I placed the book behind me and went on to the next pressing need.[8]

In all his writing one witnesses the stamp of the nonegregious, wholesome perfectionist. His honesty, intelligence, intuitiveness and passion always impress. It is more than sentimental tribute for this reader to admit to having been enticed to multiple read-overs and prolonged savoring of astonishing phrases of unsurpassed beauty, incisive sentences of poignancy, deep meaning and hard-hitting truth.

"Anointed" is a perfectly appropriate adjective and, at times, indispensable. But today everything and everyone are so "anointed," "truly anointed" or "so-o-o-o anointed" -- mainly by the lips of well-meaning, witless charismatics -- that the term is regrettably getting shoved closer to the "trite" heap. Heaven forbid! Before "anointed" is "done to death" it must quickly be applied to Stanely Jones' entire output because it fits. His writings literally throb with fresh anointing which does not fade with the passage of time. "Anointed" is the best word this writer knows that captures his authorship. "Stimulus of Christ" (See Philippians 4:13Moffatt.) is another apt phrase eloquently characterizing Stanely Jones written legacy. The two expressions are after all akin and both are hallmarks of Stanely Jones the man and writer.

Perhaps Stanley Jones impresses most by his profound sense of the relevant, especially, although not solely, in the domain of Holy Scripture. "Without conscious effort"[9] on his part, all that Stanley Jones thought and lived through the years came together around two Biblical foci -- "the Kingdom of God and the Person of Christ, the Order and the Person, the Social and the Personal."[10] Jesus' injunctive to "Seek first the Kingdom of God." did not fall on deaf ears or infertile soil in the case of this Kingdom disciple. He made it the rally cry of his heart, the "aim and goal of life," "the master-light of all our seeing."[11] As Soren Kierkegaard might have put it, he lived his life willing to will one thing only, the Kingdom of God. With the force of his entire being Stanley Jones believed that...

> The Kingdom is to be first and everything else, yes, everything else, is to be secondary and subordinate. If we do that, Jesus says, 'All things shall be added unto you.' Everything we need for life and development and happiness will be added. And that 'everything' includes the material. And not only includes it, but definitely specifies it. [One wonders, can this clarification of 'everything-including-the-material' be taken as an okay to ring the bells for the much-maligned "prosperity" gospelteers? If not entirely justified, perhaps they've been seconded by God's best Methodist missionary.] But we are seeking other things first, hence life is turning to ashes on our hands through misuse. We feverishly produce for other than Kingdom-of-God motives, and then our goods rot in our warehouses with no motive for distribution; or, when they are distributed, they become the center and source of war in a fierce struggle for markets. We are seeking first the Kingdom of Mammon, and all these things are being subtracted from us. We waste in a few years of war what we have feverishly accumulated, and more: we burden ourselves with debts for generations to come. You cannot live life against God and yourself and get away with it. The flaming tongues of belching cannon firing from their open mouths the burned bread of the people proclaim this fact in eloquent tones. All these things are being subtracted from us, and we shall eat the bitter bread of poverty and ruin because we sought other things first. 'All things betray thee which betrayeth Me.'[12]

It cannot be overly emphasized that Stanley Jones' teaching on the Kingdom of God is *the* watershed through which we must pass on the road to recovering the very thing Jesus equated with "the Final Way of Life," the Kingdom of God.[13]

The Kingdom As Key to Healing and Unity

We are convinced that Stanley Jones' scintillating and dynamic exposition of the Kingdom of God most closely parallels Jesus' own revelation of the reality, nature, laws, principles and attitudes of God's Perfect Order and of Himself as the Perfect embodiment of Divine Absolute Reign. The Kingdom of God conception so faithfully expounded by Stanley Jones, who more than anyone understood its absolute primacy and supremacy, is the heart of our task. If healing of the two crippled wings which we've identified in the Body of Christ is ever to begin, then those believers who read this book must be persuaded and gripped by the Kingdom of God, rightly understood, as absolutely crucial and decisive for our stated purposes. To sputter and to falter here is to fail dismally.

If it can be argued that down the years some "strange omission has taken place in regard to the Kingdom of God"[14] and that the Church is still subservient to the deceiving spirit that has been allowed to perpetuate this omission with the cumulative result being a sorry legacy of division, then it is past high time that the Kingdom is rediscovered. Stanley Jones puts the case starkly: "No wonder the Church has stumbled from problem to problem when its supreme value was lost or only marginally held. The Church will never get straightened out until it puts the Kingdom where Jesus put it... -- the first consideration and the first allegiance."[15]

Will this stinging indictment delivered almost fifty years ago cause nary a ripple in the Church so enamored of its separation from itself? In the current momentous push, enlisting virtually every single faith fellowship worldwide, to "Evangelize the world now!" will the Kingdom of God, the precise "motif running through everything Jesus taught"[16] still have to settle for the periphery as far as the Church's vision of these "last days" times is concerned? Like the deluded emperor, exposed through his imaginary clothes, will the Church clothe itself in a transparent, frothy adventism that keeps the Kingdom "beyond the borders of this life, a heavenly Kingdom"[17] only and fail to reclothe itself in its "rightful mind," in a sound singleminded garment of wholeness? Is this rash supposition or is it impending realism? Almost fifty years later and still telling it like it is, Stanley Jones further indicts the Church: "The Kingdom of God and the Holy Spirit are the two missing notes in much of our Christianity. And Jesus made both of them central -- one the pattern, the other the power."[18]

With the aid of such penetrating perspective as Stanley Jones exhibits throughout his relevant writings on the Kingdom, we shall endeavor to rediscover: l) why Jesus made the Kingdom central and 2) what the Kingdom of God consists of or what it looks like. The preliminary goal in this approach is to see clearly why the imperative remains for us to do no less than to realign our individual and corporate lives squarely with the Unshakable Kingdom and the Unchangeable Person.

Prologue to Understanding the Kingdom of God

A Song of Ascents, Stanley Jones' spiritual autobiography written in 1968, sounds a sad pronouncement with an all-too-accustomed ring: "For one of the greatest single hindrances, if not the greatest, to the spread of the Gospel is the divided state of Christendom."[19] A lifetime of similar statements from many aggrieved voices from every conceivable corner of the Church world have tired and tried us and jaded our private and corporate attitudes so that with one spiritless voice of indifference we reply, "What else is new?" Unfortunately, we see no solid evidence or dramatic development to contradict Stanley Jones' -- and others' -- commentary on the state of Christ's Church. In order to move the two segregated sides toward purposeful confrontation and, in turn, to stimulate the healing process between them, we see no real alternative but to try to entice the estranged parties toward serious reconsideration of and close encounter with the Kingdom of God. This is our ultimate end.

At this point we frankly warn the reader that what follows is a practically uninterrupted -- if not entirely unedited -- heavy outpouring of the Kingdom of God a la this tireless and unselfish devotee of Christ and His Kingdom. That the preponderance of this chapter must be devoted to this outstanding Christian servant's understanding of the Kingdom of God will, we trust, become cogent and compelling as the writing progresses and momentum for our stated purpose builds. With reader patience and indulgence, the fruit or payoff of this particular chapter will be evident in the final chapter as the Kingdom of God is applied as heuristic standard and corrective for what ails the paradigmatic parties of Christian disunity. In the meanwhile, the good, strong meat of this chapter centering on the "master-conception" or "master-cause," as Stanley Jones labelled the Kingdom of God in *Is the Kingdom of God Realism?*[20] cannot fail to edify and to enlarge one's vision and appreciation for timeless, universal truth.

In *The Choice Before Us* (1937) one is intrigued to see the modest way Stanley Jones introduced his beloved Kingdom. Juxtaposed to what, in the dismal thirties, was viewed as "the two great modern attempts to bring unity back into life,"[21] namely, Naziism and Fascism on the one hand and Communism on the other, the Kingdom of God was characterized as "the third attempt at unity."[22] Our Kingdom proponent writes, "The third attempt at unity was launched by the Carpenter of Nazareth on the basis that God is our Father, therefore all men are brothers, the world is a human family and the family spirit which is the spirit of cooperation must be universalized. He summed it up as the Kingdom of God on earth."[23] Of course the Kingdom of God concept was in Stanley Jones' mind infinitely more than an attempt to unify life or an alternative to the failed gods of the two terrible "isms."

In the same context Stanley Jones charged that the Christ spirit had been "betrayed by his followers"[24] and that the Kingdom of God as "universal principle of unity" had been "smothered in a mass of irrelevances and localisms..."[25] In short, it had become through gross neglect "an outworn relic."[26] Not one for pessimism, Stanley Jones sensed that the "all-comprehending principle and power for unity," which his world craved, was "becoming a new living issue."[27] Confidently he announced that his once "buried idea," this "Man and His Kingdom" were making a come back.[28] Not contenting himself with documenting damage done to the Kingdom idea, he assumed the role of harbinger of its restoration:

> It is experiencing nothing less than a resurrection... The world is hungry for something .. so universal that it takes in every human relationship and gives purpose and meaning to the whole, and something so intimate that it takes in one's own personal need and meets it with redemption and power by which to live. Is the Kingdom of God that conception? We think so.[29]

It is extremely ironic that the exuberance with which Stanley Jones heralded the Kingdom of God as *the* burning issue confronting Christianity and the world in the dark days preceding World War II sent a rumbling reverberation through the corridor of time which ended up not as resolute rejoicing but as a hollow whimper on the cold modern doorstep of a fragmented Christendom. Where is the rebirth of the Kingdom Stanley Jones predicted? Where is that "central rock by which everything else is held up?"[30] Why is it no more axiomatic today than it was when Stanley Jones first began to rescue and reinterpret the Kingdom of God into reality? How much longer must the Kingdom of God be distorted and subordinated amid glitzy theological trifles and acculturated predispositions of the personal versus the social schools and sequestered out of its central relevancy and potency? How much longer will the Church continue to take away the teaching of the Kingdom thereby flattening out the teaching of Jesus "to the level of other teachers"?[31]

Stanley Jones insisted that Kingdom teaching "makes Him [Jesus] stand out."[32] The Kingdom of God is the centerpiece of the religion of Christ providing the social order with stability without which that religion "would utterly flounder."[33] The world prior to World War II demanded social and economic justice; the world today demands no less. A way of "personal deliverance only ... would be entirely inadequate."[34] To drive the point home as hard as possible, Stanley Jones allows the Kingdom to adjudicate for the decayed inner life of the individual and the insecure social order that has broken down under its "own inner strains and contradictions."[35] According to Stanley Jones, modern man...

> feels the need of something that will put foundation under the social order and give him the sense that he has the basis for a corporate life that will not fluctuate between wild hope and black despair. The modern man is thus doubly hurt and needs a double remedy -- something that will give him a reconstructed inner life and will also give him a new basis for a decaying social and economic order. I can be obsessed with nothing less than that which meets that double need. Much of religion does not, hence I have lost interest in such religion.[36]

The Kingdom of God opened itself up to Stanley Jones not because he determined to study and master it. On the contrary, he surrendered to it, eagerly expectant and determined to follow it, to live it, to become it "in miniature."[37] Called by H. G. Wells "the most astonishing proposition ever presented to the mind of man,"[38] the Kingdom of God was the thing that Jesus made "central, formative, all-important."[39] It was the thing he emphasized in the beginning of his ministry, "Repent, for the kingdom of heaven is at hand." And for forty days after the resurrection he spoke to his disciples concerning the Kingdom of God. Stanley Jones says, "Between the forty days of temptation when the whole question at issue was the methods by which the Kingdom was to be brought in and the forty days of postresurrection teaching the theme was one -- the Kingdom."[40]

Jesus used "simile, metaphor, parable, and direct statement to interpret"[41] the "simplest" and yet "profoundest idea ever offered to man."[42] Of the almost ineffable dilemma Stanley Jones says, "...words broke down under the weight of new meaning -- the conception was bigger than the vehicle of expression, for the eternal was breaking into time."[43] By his own account, Stanley Jones would seem to apprehend the Kingdom only to experience its elusive powers. He writes candidly, "You think you have got its full meaning and then it breaks out beyond you and you are a learner again. Enfolded into the very texture of things it is yet unfolding as we learn and morally respond to it."[44]

Jesus spoke of the Kingdom as something "open" and yet "secret" (See Luke 8:10). It is "...something you have and yet something that is still secret, hidden but unfolding."[45] With keen psychological insight and spiritual acumen, Stanley Jones intuits that "Man needs nothing so much as something he has got and yet hasn't got, something that satisfies him and yet keeps him forever on the stretch for more."[46] However, it should be noted that balance to what Stanley Jones calls, potential "snare" and "delusion," "mystery" and "moonshine" is not lacking within the Kingdom idea. It is "sufficiently graspable to provide a program for action now."[47]

The Concept of the Kingdom of God

What has been written thus far, in what might be construed as tedious, protracted prologue, is a deliberate, unhesitating attempt to convey the utter importance of the Kingdom of God concept and of Stanley Jones' singular, special relationship to it. Only if this exercise is thoroughgoing will it be possible to make a convincing case for appropriation and application of Kingdom truth and of Stanley Jones' swift insights into Kingdom principles for the task of effecting synthesis and reconciliation of the disparate factions under consideration.

Perhaps a reminder regarding the expression "Kingdom concept" is needed here. Such usage as Kingdom concept, conception, idea, ideal, fact, reality and the like is unavoidable for analytical, communicative and literary purposes. But such distinction in and interchange of terms should not cloud the issue nor imply apparent contradiction. Of course, the Kingdom of God is not mere "concept," for Jesus presented the Kingdom as "fact -- the supreme fact of life."[48] Moreover, Stanley Jones points out that the Kingdom of God is "social fact."[49] Near the end of his instructive explication of what it means to be renounced in spirit -- the end of which is receptivity, self-realization and world-participation -- Stanley Jones quotes the Christ of the Mount: "'Deathless and happy is the man who is renounced in spirit, his is the kingdom of heaven ["his is life"].'" (See Matthew 5:3-12Moffatt).[50] Then he says, "Everything belongs to the man who wants nothing. Having nothing, he possesses all things in life, including life itself. Nothing will be denied the man who denies *himself*. Having chosen to be utterly solitary, he now comes into possession of the most utterly social fact in the universe, the kingdom of God."[51]

The fact that the Kingdom of God is "fact" and "*social* fact" is not incidental. Neither is the intertwining of the content of the so-called Sermon on the Mount with the Kingdom of God. The two belong inextricably together. The affirmation that Christ never presented an idea -- whether in the guise of the message of the mount or the Kingdom of God -- that wasn't operative permeates the critical book, *Is the Kingdom of God Realism?* The rhetorical question posed by this title imples that the gospel of Jesus Christ, the message he gave, his way of facing life were realistic. That gospel, that message, that way of facing life, according to Stanley Jones, was the Kingdom of God. "It was the center and circumference of all He taught and did. It was His gospel: 'Jesus went ... preaching the gosepl of the kingdom.'"[52]

Stanley Jones taught that Jesus was not a moralist "imposing ... a [moral] code for which humanity is badly made," but a "revealer of reality."[53] He also held that Jesus was the "simplification of God."[54] As the great Revealer and Simplification of God how does Jesus define the Kingdom of God? Stanley Jones directs us to the Lord's Prayer:

> "Thy kingdom come. Thy will be done in earth, as it is in heaven." The second phrase explains the first -- the Kingdom of God is the doing of the will of God on earth as it is done in heaven. And how would the will of God be done in heaven? Partially, in certain departments of life? In the individual, but not in the social arrangements, the collective set-up? To ask such questions is to answer them. Obviously, the whole of life must come under the single sway, nothing must be left out, it must be totalitarian, utterly so. The Kingdom of God is the master-conception, the master-plan, the master-purpose, the

> master-will that gathers everything up into itself and gives it redemption, coherence, purpose, goal.[55]

The Kingdom Is Both Personal and Social

Stanley Jones provides this glimpse of the Hebraic notion of the Kingdom which Jesus inherited and which gives historical perspective to the meaning which Jesus attached to the Kingdom.

> Their nation as a nation was to come under a new sovereignty, the Kingdom of God, and they were to express it in their corporate life. It was fundamentally a social conception. If Jesus made it into a personal conception as well -- the individual entering it by a new birth and embodying it in a personal expression -- nevertheless this was only a corrective to the over-socialized conception the Hebrews held of the Kingdom. If Jesus made it personal, He nevertheless retained the fundamentally social side of it. That was the taken-for-granted side of it present in the minds of the hearers. We of the modern day, without that inheritance of a social conception of the Kingdom, reading the New Testament with its personal emphasis regarding the Kingdom, miss the point entirely if we do not put ourselves in the place of the hearers of Jesus' message and realize that His personal emphases were only correctives and were not the whole story. This is where the Church has gone fundamentally astray regarding the Kingdom. It has forgotten that background. Jesus was not teaching the world, He was teaching His own people and He was correcting false ideas as well as imparting new ones. But the fundamental social content of the Kingdom was the basic starting point -- the nation and the individual were to embody it. The teaching of Jesus seemed, then, to be this: the entrance into the Kingdom of God is individual and by a new birth, but the nature of the Kingdom is social.[56]

This necessary corrective leads Stanley Jones to conclude that Jesus was presenting a new Order, "God's Order standing at the door of the lower order ready to replace it." He clarifies further,

> This higher Order is founded on redemption, love, mutual aid, justice, and a fair opportunity to everyone. This higher Order confronts this lower order founded on greed, selfishness, and exploitation with its consequent strife and confusion. It is God's Order over against man's system. This new Order breaks into the individual and the collective will wherever consent is given. It is the Final Way of Life offered to our expediences.[57]

At the beginning of this chapter we spoke of the Kingdom of God as Life. More needs to be said to clarify this claim put forth by Stanley Jones throughout his writings.

> Jesus made "the Kingdom" and "life" synonymous. He used them interchangeably. "It is better for thee to enter into life maimed." ... "It is better for thee to enter into the kingdom of God with one eye." (Mark 9:43, 47) The Kingdom is Life with a capital 'L' -- Life as it ought to be. .... But the Kingdom is not only Life, it is the redemption of life. Jesus uses the Kingdom and redemption interchangeably in parallel passages. "Your redemption draweth nigh," ... "the kingdom of God draweth nigh," The Kingdom, then, is not only Life, but it is the redemption of life. If it were only Life, it would paralyze us with its overwhelming greatness and purity. But it does more than overwhelm -- it helps us to overcome. It gives us standards, but it also gives us salvation.[58]

But not only are we shown that the Kingdom and Life -- real Life, not half-living -- are the same but that Jesus and the Kingdom are identical.

> ...yet one has to turn to Christ Himself for the meaning of the Kingdom. For he presented Himself as the Kingdom personalized. He identified Himself with the Kingdom. .... As He is the Incarnation of God, so He is the Incarnation of the Reign of God. .... He made "for my sake" and "for the Kingdom's sake" synonymous. When Jesus stood before Pilate, He did not say, "the Kingdom of God," but "My Kingdom" -- He put Himself and the Kingdom together -- in Him they had coalesced and were one. The Supreme Order and the Supreme Person meet and are one. This makes our religion at once social and personal, for to have relationship with Chirst is to have relationship with the new Order embodied in Christ. .... God not only redeems in terms of Christ, and through Christ, He rules in terms of Christ, and through Christ -- the Kingdom is the Christ spirit regnant.[59]

The meaning and nature of the Kingdom as exposed by Stanley Jones can only be presented in bare outline in this context. But it is incumbent on us to make stick the point of Jesus' appearing not just as an individual but as the embodiment of the Cause of Causes, the Kingdom of God.[60] If repetition will do the job for us it is best to repeat in summary fashion. What was needed in Jesus' day is the need now. We need no less than ...

an all-inclusive Order which shall gather up into itself the lesser meanings and loyalties of life and give coherence and purpose to the whole. Nothing less than a Universal Order can do this. The only Universal Order is the Kingdom of God.

But only a Universal Person can embody a Universal Order. Only the Son of man can embody the hopes and longings of the sons of men. Christ as the Son of man, the Universal Man, embodied in Himself the Universal Order, the Kingdom of God. The Universal Person and the Universal Cause met and were one.

Jesus was the Key to that Kingdom. Just as Jesus reveals the nature of God, He reveals the nature of the reign of God. The Kingdom of God is Christlikeness universalized. God reigns in the spirit that Jesus reigns, and with the same weapons of coercion, the coercion of the Cross. This is important, for many still conceive of God beating down His enemies by force and establishing His reign. If Jesus is kept as the Key, then this force-conception of the Kingdom fades out and the Cross, as the working force, becomes dominant. ....

This, then, was the gospel: God's absolute Order embodied in an absolute Person confronts us with its redemptive offer and demand. It is not an impersonal Order confronting us, but an Order that looks out from tender eyes -- the Order is warm and human.[61]

To get in focus the picture of the Kingdom as sketched so far, as personalized, as social, as Life with a capital 'L', and so on, we note the following summary statements:

1) A Kingdom presented in a Person who remakes other persons, and these persons who accept it and live by it in individual and collective living find that this is Life.[62]
2) But Christ makes Himself synonymous with Life: 'I am ... Life;' if Christ is Life and the Kingdom is Life, then Christ and the Kingdom are one.[63]
3) The Kingdom is redemption for the individual and for the whole of society, and the Kingdom is Life and meets us in the Person of Christ.[64]
4) The Absolute Order meets us in the Absolute Person and the obligation laid on us is absolute -- 'Surrender.' In surrendering we find ourselvs in obedience to the final way of life.[65]

Anticipating a possible misconception in the matter of the Kingdom's being an "all-inclusive" and "all-pervasive"[66] or "all-enveloping and "all-penetrating"[67] Order, Stanley Jones says,

...we are not identifying the Kingdom with the sum total of tangible things. The Kingdom is transcendent as well as immanent; it is built within the foundation of the world but it is also invading the world. Jesus said, "The Kingdom of God is within you," and yet He also said, "It is at your doors." The Kingdom is the divine invasion and the divine immanence. It is beyond Time, an eternal Kingdom, and yet it functions within Time. It is above History and yet it works within History. It is in Time and yet will never come completely within Time for the eternal cannot be fully packed within the Time process.[68]

The Nazareth Manifesto

Next we turn to an overview of the content Jesus put into the Kingdom concept via the Nazareth manifesto:

'The Spirit of the Lord is upon me,
Because he anointed me to preach good tidings to the poor [the economically disinherited];
He hath sent me to proclaim release to the captives [the socially and politically disinherited];
And recovering of sight to the blind [the physically disinherited];
To set at liberty them that are bruised [the morally and spiritually disinherited];
To proclaim the acceptable year of the Lord [the Lord's year of Jubilee (a new world beginning)].'[69]

Stanley Jones draws our attention to this program of reconstruction designed to "meet the sum total of human need."[70] Relative to the first specific, "Good news to the poor," Stanley Jones asks, "What would be good news to the poor? To make them content in their poverty?" The answer he supplies is infinite sense: "Poverty can be banished. .... Poverty is not God's will; it is ours." The caution is made in the second specific, "Release to the captives," not to overly spiritualize. Jesus is referring to the "total captivity of man. .... The Kingdom would stop all exploitation and make man an end in himself, as the child of God. .... The underlying foundation ideas of the Kingdom would work out in the ending of all exploitation and bondage of every type and kind." As to the third specific, Stanley Jones says simply,

Disease is not God's will. Jesus never asked men to bear it as the will of God. The Kingdom is an offensive against it. For the Kingdom stands for life to the full. Sin, error, disease, and death are anti-life, so the Kingdom is on an offensive against them. Jesus did not cure disease to show His power, or to validate His claims as Messiah; He cured disease because men needed to be cured. It was a part of the redemptive purpose of God. Healing, therefore, was not a bait for evangelism -- it was evangelism applied to the physical. It stands in its own right as a part of the coming of the Kingdom.[71]

Those televangelists and teachers who often erroneously and vociferously charge that too much "traditional Christianity" and too many segments of the Church in general have been against healing could do worse than read Stanley Jones' books for solid evidence to the contrary and proper insight into this particular mainline churchman's beliefs and experiences, which plant him firmly on the side of the total ministry of Jesus and of the New Testament.

The fourth item, "The setting at liberty of them that are bruised," is dealt with thusly: It is seen to be referring to "the moral and spiritual needs of men" from the translation from the Aramaic, "'To strengthen with forgiveness them that are bruised.'" We see here a very humane and sensitive insight into that which bruises soul (mind, will, emotions) and spirit:

[Ours] is a world of moral consequence. We hurt ourselves upon the moral facts of the universe. We do not break the laws of God, they break us. Our spirits are bruised and hurt. Nothing can lift those bruises except forgiveness -- the forgiveness of God. Man needs nothing so much as he needs to know that he is reconciled to God and the moral law. The Kingdom offers a new birth, a fresh start. Some of our difficulties of human living are in the economic, some in the social and political, some in the physical, but some are within us, in our own wrong selves. Give a man everything he needs in the economic, social, political and the physical, and yet you have not healed him unless you heal him at the heart. The new birth gives that healing. It strikes at man's deepest and most fundamental need. .... It reconciles man at the heart of things to the Heart of Things.[72]

Finally, the fifth item is amplified in these resounding words:

Jesus took this conception, [the Lord's Year of Jubilee (a fresh world beginning)] enlarged and universalized it and put it at the heart of His program. .... As the Jewish Year of Jubilee worked from the social order to the individual, so this item in the program of Jesus does the same. .... [The Christian is not confined to] working from the individual to the social order.[73]

With the inherent force of the new world order, the Christian is enabled to work from both directions "-- from the individual to the social order [impacting the social order] and from the social order to the individual [changing the individual through changing the social order.]."[74]

Here we have both the content -- "a reconstruction which would extend through the economic, the social, the political, the physical, the spiritual, and to the total order" -- and the *dynamic* of operation -- "the redemptive Spirit of God working directly and through every right agency" -- of the Kingdom as Jesus disclosed it.[75] Stanley Jones favored this synopsis of Jesus' stance toward the Kingdom as set forth by Professor Ernest F. Scott:

1. Jesus took over the Jewish apocalyptic hope of a new age coming.
2. The Kingdom stands for the higher spiritual order which lies behind the material world and gives it meaning. A consummation will come in which it will be fully manifest, but God is reigning now.
3. While the Kingdom includes all higher reality, it stands more especially for the moral order. It means the perfect fulfillment of that will of God which under earthly conditions can only be dimly apprehended.
4. The Kingdom is realized in the inward life of fellowship with God.
5. The Kingdom implies a community of God's people and is thus social as well as moral and spiritual.[76]

Thus, we have the message of Jesus encapsulated in this outline. Moreover, Jesus taught that the Kingdom is both "within you" and "in the midst of you." It is also "at our doors" in readiness to "break into the total life in redemptive power." If the Kingdom of God, as Jesus, announced, is "come upon you," then it is not only "within us" or "in our midst" but is poised to press upon us "to displace the lower order with God's order."[77]

It is obviously wrong and presumptuous to suppose that the thoroughly lucid insights and remarkably penetrating analyses which we've lifted from Stanley Jones' books could possibly exhaust the Kingdom of God concept and render it "defined." But this meager distillation of major thoughts must end for the sake of space constraints despite the temptation to include every possible facet of Sanley Jones' theology. We are pressed to wind up (down?) this chapter by spotlighting a few additional, essential considerations about the Kingdom.

Other Aspects of the Kingdom

The Kingdom of God was the "central rock" in Jesus' life and teaching "by which everything else is held up." Without the underpinning of the Kingdom "the teaching of Jesus flattens out to a great extent to the level of other teachers."[78] Without the Kingdom of God there would be no "social order" in the "religion of Chirst" to put under the world's "toppling order[s]." Stanley Jones correctly observes that this being the case -- Jesus' teachings minus the Kingdom -- "*It would be a way of personal deliverance only and as such would be entirely inadequate*." [My emphasis].[79] Relative to this important assertion, we see the counterbalance in these words:

> The Kingdom of God is the most intense social order with the most intense heightening of the individual worth. These two apparently incompatibles were in a living blend.[80] The putting together of a strong social order and individual liberty is one of the most difficult things on earth, and yet it was done naturally and noramlly in the Kingdom-of-God Order.[81]

We dare not gloss over this vital truth that "inherent in the teaching and spirit of Jesus"[82] individual liberty coupled with social consciousness was inherently there in the Kingdom of God. The Kingdom of God disallows any divorce of the individual from the social. Stanley Jones guides us in this reasoned response: "'The Community does not exist in and for itself, nor does the individual. Both exist in and for each other and neither can exist without the other. The ultimate fact of social existence is personality in community.'" He goes on to say,

> And it is there wherever this Kingdom-of-God life is experienced. The moment one comes in contact with Christ a strong social sense is at once aroused. It needs only to be channeled to make a new earth. It has lacked that channeling and hence has run into a great deal of sentimentalism. But channeled or unchanneled it is there as an integral part of one's experience of Christ.[83]

Always scrupulous in balancing one side of the argument with its opposite point, Stanley Jones allows for the "sense of individual liberty that has to be experienced to be known"[84] when one encounters Christ. With deep conviction and convincing tones he says,

> I do not argue but I only testify that the more I belong to Christ the more I am my very own. The soul seems universalized and everything seems to belong to it, including itself. There is a sense of freedom that is profound, for the Kingdom of God is the soul's native land, and where we find it we breathe the air of freedom and at-homeness. We are made for this as the lungs are made for air. It is therefore an ultimate way to live.[85]

Time and again we are brought to the realization that "Jesus intended the Kingdom to be a new society as well as a personal reign of God in the heart."[86] This is seen in the fact that

> after appealing in vain to the Hebrew nation to embody it, [Jesus] said, 'The kingdom of God shall be taken away from you, and given to a nation bringing forth the fruits thereof.' This plainly shows that the corporate society -- the nation -- as well as the individual was to embody it. It shows also that the Kingdom was to get into the national structure as intimately as the life of a tree is in the structure of the tree, so that 'the fruits' of the Kingdom are a natural, normal result.[87]

As to the fruits of the Kingdom Stanley Jones boldly declares that

> in a national life [they] would be that which would grow out of life organized around love. The national life is usually organized around the hunger motive with the love motive subservient, softening the hunger motive here and there. The consequence is that we have a jungle civilization, 'the fruits' of which are strain, strife, and final war. This is inherent in our present system, for it is organized on the basis of ruthless competition. The Kingdom would organize life around love. Competition would be converted. It would be harnessed to the collective good. We should still compete in a Kingdom society, but it would be a friendly competition as to who could give most to the collective good. This would mean that the impetus and drive coming from competition would no longer be destructive and disruptive as it now is, for it is now harnessed to selfishness, but would be constructive and contributive. The more we would compete, the more we would complete. It would not be a struggle for life, but a struggle for

the life of others.[88]

As noted above the *dynamic* behind the whole Kingdom is the Spirit of the Lord. (See Luke 4:18). It follows, therefore, that the methods of bringing in this new Order of God ought to be true to the Spirit of Christ -- not to the spirit of conventional wisdom, nor to the spirit of prevailing cultural or political views, nor to the spirit of popularized lukewarm religiosity or churchianity -- as some have labeled it -- that tends to accomodate the status quo. Stanley Jones explicitly calls for methods which are consistent with the Christ Spirit and means which are consistent with "the end in view."[89] To insist on Christlike methods and means is important and perforce "rules out for the Christian the method of force and war."[90] Rules out force and war because...

> if you should bring in the Kingdom by compulsion, then when you got it, it would not be the Kingdom -- it would be something else. It would have been lost by the very methods used to bring it in. That Jesus used only moral compulsion may be seen in the cleansing of the Temple. The whip-cords were used not on men, but on the sheep and cattle: 'Making a scourge of cords, he drove them all, sheep and cattle together, out of the temple,' (John 2.15, Moffatt). Regarding the men involved, it was a *moral* compulsion -- not immoral as war and coercion are. The Christian believes in force consistent with the spirit of Christ. That would allow a police force and rule out militarism. The difference is obvious: a police force brings the culprit before a bar of justice, to be judged by a tribunal of right. Armies trained for war bring guilty and innocent alike before the tribunal of force to be judged by the question of might.
>
> But the Spirit of the Lord as the dynamic would also mean the Spirit of God working through the moral facts of the universe, through the discoveries of science, through the make-up of our sociological order, through the illuminations coming to the enlightened minds of men of good will, and through the direct operation of the Spirit of God upon individuals. The Spirit of God as the dynamic would mean that the very stars in their courses would work in behalf of this new Kingdom, and conversely that these very stars would work for the overthrow of every kingdom founded on other principles.[91]

We include the above passage, simply staggering in its refreshing honesty, for one primary reason. It helps to orient us toward our preliminary task in the upcoming chapters of confronting the Church in general and our two historically antagonistic traditions in particular with avoiding, reducing and failing to take seriously the Kingdom message and mandate and the ensuing detrimental effect such sins of omission have had on the life, witness and mission of the Body of Christ for nearly two millennia.

Still outstanding are several decisive assumptions about the Kingdom which must at least be mentioned before we can in good conscience conclude this chapter. As the Kingdom "prepared for us from the foundation of the world"[92] it is definitely not "an after-thought imposed on life, rather it is written in the very constitution of things, in the very make-up of our universes, and of our being."[93]

With acute sensitivity to scriptures Stanley Jones reminds us that we are told in the New Testament to *see* the Kingdom, *receive* it, *enter into* it, and *proclaim* it.[94] According to the New Testament and to Stanley Jones the idea of "building the Kingdom" is anathema. Two cogent reasons are offered: 1) The Kingdom is already there, in existence, to be received as fact. It distorts Biblical doctrine and defies logic to assume we are to "bring into life," or to try to "produce" or to "construct" something that is already there.[95] Stanley Jones says plainly, "We are to build the Church, but not the Kingdom, for the Church is a relativism built more or less after the pattern of the absolute, the Kingdom of God."[96] Without trying to "one up" Stanley Jones, but with Jesus' declaration to Peter and the other disciples ringing in the ear, perhaps we need to amend this opening line slightly to read: "We accede to the Lord, who will build His Church, utilizing us or laying us aside as He sees fit." 2) We are not to build the Kingdom. Rather, we are to build the Church after the pattern of the Absolute Person and His Absolute Order.

No more straightforward, nor critical offer has come to us than to see, to receive, to enter into and to proclaim the Kingdom of God. The only requirement is the child's capacity for total surrender and receptivity. To the grim fact that there is evidence of failure to receive, Stanley Jones adds these sobering words:

> That men do not 'receive' the Kingdom does not say the Kingdom is not present. God has never abdicated. He rules. But whether men 'receive' that rule is another question. If they do not receive it, then all the worse for them, for the Kingdom then operates in self-frustration and self-destruction. Men hurt themselves if they do not receive the Kingdom. The law of gravity has always been here and men have pro-

> gressed only as they have accommodated themselves to that fact, have obeyed the law. Whey they obeyed it, they did not 'build' the law of gravity, they simply 'received' it, received what was an existing fact. And they had to receive it 'as a little child,' had to give up all preconceived notions, had to sit down before the facts as a little child and be willing to follow to whatever ends nature leads them or they would know nothing.[97]

In other words, when we work its laws and cooperate with its principles and goals the Kingdom works and cooperates with us, not against us. Its opposite is set forth in the recapitulated Eden story as reminder that we cannot "work against the structure of our being and get away with it."[98] This "living against" constitutes sin. Sin is construed as

> an attempt to live against the laws of your own being and get away with it. The long history of mankind written in blood and tears tells one thing and one thing alone! It can't be done -- the soul that sinneth does die. Here and now it dies -- the bloom of life withers, something inwardly snaps, the machinery of life tries to work against itself and succeeds in destroying itself.[99]

Taking pains to expose its egregious mislabeling, Stanley Jones irrefutably shows that sin is not *natural.* If it were natural, "when we commit it we would feel inwardly fulfilled, at home with ourselves and with the universe."[100] Quite the reverse, "we feel ill at ease, estranged, inwardly outraged. This shows it is not natural -- the thing for which nature is made."[101] Emphatically, he states that sin is literally "'missing the mark,' missing the thing for which you are made, an attempt to make yourself do something for which you are not made."[102] Before we depart the subject of sin as anti-Kingdom living, if, indeeed, it can be called living, we feel impelled to offer a corrective to those who fling about the term "natural" in relation to sin when what they really mean is "accustomed." We "accustom" ourselves to sin; it is not natural to our being otherwise we would thrive under it. "Natural" is also blatantly misused in quoting certain versions of scripture passages where that word has appeared in these dubious passages when the more meaningful and appropriate word, "unspiritual," should have appeared. The "natural" being is not pejorative in the economy of the Kindom. Jesus came to take away the unnatural things that corrupt our being -- sin, error, disease, death -- and to replace them with goodness, truth, health and life. These latter four "natural" things are the mainfestations of the Kingdom of God -- "the Kingdom of God functioning within us, making us natural, making us healthy. We are no longer 'missing the mark,' we are 'hitting the mark.' We find that life will work in God's way and in no other."[103]

On the topic of the Kingdom's coming, Stanley Jones derives three phases from the Scriptures. **"HE WHO IS AND WAS AND IS COMING.** (Revelation 1.4, Moffatt)."[104] He points out that special attention shoud be paid to the *is coming* because Jesus primarily *is*. "Christ embodies this Kingdom 'is' -- He is a present, all-enveloping, all-penetrating, inescapable Fact, the Great Contemporary. It is so with the Kingdom."[105] While Jesus was emphatic about the catastrophic, apocalyptic coming of the Kingdom He did not overlook its gradualistic mode,[106] nor did he "despise the quiet unobtrusive coming of that Kingdom in individual acceptance and in corporate permeation."[107] Almost in antiphonal, litany-like expressiveness, Stanley Jones underscores the harmonic balance of Jesus' teaching on the phases of the Kingdom. He writes, "His realism is seen when He taught that the Kingdom is coming like lightning and coming like leaven, coming like a blast and growing like a blade, coming with 'power and great glory,' and yet as unobtrusive and tiny as a grain of mustard seed -- and as growing![108]

Described as the 'Great Consummation' the Kingdom is coming but "primarily and fundamentally the Kingdom *is*."[109] Stanley Jones admits to being awestruck in realizing that the Kingdom of God really is within us, that it is the moral law of our being,[110] and that it is not an idealism "which you can take or not take and nothing much will happen, that you might not get a reward in heaven by and by, but here and now life will go on undistrubed..." Although we have already sounded the warning against the Kingdom of God as idealism earlier in this chapter, it bears repeating in this amplification., Put bluntly, "[y]ou can dodge an ideal, but you cannot dodge yourself. When you default against the Kingdom, you default against yourself, for that Kingdom is written in your very makeup. The Kingdom *is*."[111]

The Church and the Kingdom

What about the Church? Where does it fit into the overarching scheme of Kingdom reality? Is it less real than the Kingdom? Is the Church to be so completely overshadowed by Kingdom patterns and exigencies that it is left missionless, diminished in role, purpose and relevancy? To raise such questions borders on if not the absurd then on missing the point. The following shorthand assertions offer a distillation of Stanley Jones' crucial distinctions between the Church and the Kingdom:

1. The Church is a relativism.[112]	1. The Supreme Kingdom, the Kingdom of God is Absolute.[113]
2. Christ never made himself synonymous with the Church.[114]	2. The Kingdom and Christ are synonymous.
3. The Church may be and is the agent of redemption, of the "coming of that redemption."	3. The Kingdom is itself redemption -- "not the subject of redemption -- it offers it."[115]
4. We are to build the Church, for it is "a relativism built more or less after the pattern of the absolute, the Kingdom of God."	4. We are not to build the Kingdom for it is already built. "For this 'Kingdom is built from the foundation of the world.'"[116]

In short, there can be no true loyalty to the Church if she insists on being equal to the Kingdom or seeks to usurp it. Stanley Jones minces no words:

> I am bound to be loyal to the Church to the degree that it is loyal to the Kingdom, but my highest loyalty is to the Kingdom, and when these loyalties conflict, then I must bow the knee finally to the Kingdom. Any false loyalty to the Church which would make it take the place of the Kingdom is destructive to the Church. When we make a relative thing into an absolute, then we have idolatry. A relative order trying to act the part of an absolute order becomes a strutting impotency. As the agent of the coming of the Kingdom it is a humble potency.[117]

Perhaps all that needs to be reiterated is this essential statement that "All life is lifted by surrender to higher life."[118] Stanley Jones is correct in saying that as man surrenders himself and the kingdoms he finds himself in to the Kingdom of God, he "partakes of a higher kingdom."[119] The Church should not try to evade this Kingdom law. The Church

> ..will have to be surrendered in order to be found. It is not an absolute -- the Kingdom of God is. It is not an end -- the Kingdom of God is. Anyone who holds the Church first is guilty of idolatry. When the Church centers itself on itself, like the individual it loses itself. 'He that saveth his life shall lose it' and this means the group as well as the individual. One will never know the glory and beauty of the Church until it is surrendered to the Kingdom of God. Then it comes back to one purified and related and found. Our loyalty to our Church must bend the knee to something higher -- the Kingdom of God.[120]

Stanley Jones says that to make the Church identical to the Kingdom is "to spoil both."[121] His explanation has the ring of truth. He asks how the Church and the Kingdom can be synonymous and how the Church can be absolute when it is made up of relative elements. Even if the Church were perfect, its relativism would remain, for then it would only be relatively perfect, made up of relatively perfect beings "in the process of an eternal growth."[122]

> Hence the Church made up of growing beings, even at its best, can only be a relativism. For it must be by the very nature of things related to something higher than itself, from which it gets authority and the right to live. Only the Roman Catholic Church made the Church and the Kingdom synonymous, and this Church was therefore bound to make itself infallible. But we know that the only thing infallible about the Roman Catholic Church is that it has been infallibly fallible like the rest of us! To identify the Church and the Kingdom is to leave Christianity floundering in the midst of its relativism with no absolute order to which we can look for absolue authority, to which we can give our complete obedience.[123]

On the point of Christ's not being synonymous with the Church, Stanley Jones has the important insight into Paul's figure of the Church as the "Body of Christ" implying distinction and calling attention to the fact that "Christ was the Head of the Body -- the Head, the master; the Body, the servant." It is clear that the relationship is one of unequals. Christ as Head commands and the Body obeys. It is true that Christ "loved the Church and gave Himself for it that He might redeem it. But He never gave Himself for the Kingdom to redeem it." The difference between the Kingdom and the Church is profound.[124] As we see in Luke's gospel the Kingdom is equated with redemption: "Your redemption draweth nigh." (Luke 21:28) This ties in with the passage in Revelation (12:10, Moffatt), "Now it has come, the salvation and power, the reign ('Kingdom') of our God and the authority of his Christ!" Stanley Jones points out that it is here that the Kingdom is made synoymous with "salvation and power," underscoring again that the Kingdom is redemption.[125]

With the Kingdom of God concept as backdrop and an elucidating bird's eye view of its vital whole-life impact as distilled from E. Stanley Jones' masterful interpretation, we must now fix our attention on the Church. Quite frankly what we're about to see will be a disheartening disarray of accumulated good and bad habits (from both conscious and subconscious levels), time-laden accretions of good and bad customs, attitudes and behavior brought forth, as it were, from good and evil stores. But where distortions abound in the Church at large and within our two parties, it is our fervent prayer that courage to face up to our shortcomings, weaknesses and massive problems will come to produce an enlivened endurance that will produce changed character that will produce hope which will not disappoint. (See Romans 5:3-5). Then perhaps, by the grace of God, the unity so elusive and evasive which we so very much need will be added unto us as surprise bonus.

Notes

1. Stanley Jones allows this secret of God to unfold and flower in these words: "...the word become flesh become the Word of God become flesh become the Word of the kingdom of God become flesh." (Mathews and Mathews, 1972, p. 112).

2. Lest this exorbitant accolade cause Stanley Jones to wince and frown at us, we quickly insert his own five-word disclaimer: "It was all of grace!" (*A Song of Ascents*, p. 62). Apropos his personal acknowledgement of God's hand of grace throughout his life, in his immensely moving and revealing spiritual autobiography, *A Song of Ascents* (1968), Stanley Jones testifies of one of the many strings in his lyre with which he began his Song of Ascents -- the "string of adequacy": "I was cleansed by the Holy Spirit in both conscious and subconscious minds and unified within, and given power by that same Holy Spirit to witness for my Lord. And the

amazing thing was that I did nothing to merit all this. I did nothing but receive; the initiative was his. Love invaded me, and now love pervaded me as I began my pilgrimage from what I was to what he is making me. I was at once humbled to the dust and lifted to the highest heaven. It was all of grace!" (p. 62).

3. *The Theology and Missiology of E. Stanley Jones*, p. 63.
4. Jones, 1937, p. 19.
5. *Ibid.*, 1939, p. 174.
6. Mathews and Mathews, p. 9.
7. Jones, 1948, p. 5.
8. Mathews and Mathews, p. 9.
9. *Ibid.*
10. *Ibid.*
11. Jones, 1940, pp. 68, 69.
12. *Ibid.*
13. *Ibid.*, 1937, p. 23.
14. *Ibid.*, 1946, p. 201.
15. *Ibid.*
16. *Ibid.*
17. *Ibid.*
18. *Ibid.*
19. *Ibid.*, 1968, p. 273.
20. *Ibid.*, 1940, p. 68.
21. *Ibid.*, 1937, p. 13.
22. *Ibid.*, p. 14.
23. *Ibid.*, pp. 14-15.
24. *Ibid.*, p. 15.
25. *Ibid.*
26. *Ibid.*
27. *Ibid.*
28. *Ibid.*
29. *Ibid.*
30. *Ibid.*, p. 19.
31. *Ibid.*
32. *Ibid.*
33. *Ibid.*
34. *Ibid.*
35. *Ibid.*
36. *Ibid.*
37. *Ibid.*, p. 24.
38. *Ibid.*, p. 20.
39. *Ibid.*
40. *Ibid.*

41. *Ibid.*
42. *Ibid.*, p. 21.
43. *Ibid.*, pp. 20-21.
44. *Ibid.*, p. 21.
45. *Ibid.*
46. *Ibid.*
47. *Ibid.*, p. 22.
48. *Ibid.*, 1940, p. 63.
49. *Ibid.*, p. 1931, p. 59.
50. *Ibid.*, pp. 59, 60, 55.
51. *Ibid.*, p. 59.
52. *Ibid.*, 1940, p. 53.
53. Mathews and Mathews, p. 15. To keep us from stumbling down the dead-end road of viewing Jesus as merely a great ethicist, we find this excellent truth marker: "Jesus did not teach an ethic -- that would have made Him a moralist, teaching moral ideas. He was not a moralist teaching abstract codes of conduct. He was a proclaimer of a Kingdom -- a Kingdom of fact, not a code of morals -- and the coming of that Kingdom was the impinging of realism on unrealism, the displacing of unworkable ways with God's workable ways." (Jones, 1940, p. 61).
54. Jones, 1931, p. 27.
55. *Ibid.*, 1940, p. 53. Stanley Jones stringently warned of the "subtle danger" of slipping into the "thought of idealism" by referring to the Kingdom of God as goal or master-conception. Idealism renders the Kingdom as "distant goal," thereby sapping the "very life of the Kingdom proposal." Admitting that the Kingdom is only a goal and conception as far as we are concerned, he says, "The Kingdom itself is not a conception, but a fact. Jesus never presented the Kingdom as a conception -- that would have left it in the realm of idea. He presented it as a fact -- a fact that had to be acted on -- that left it in the realm of realism." pp. 70-71.
56. *Ibid.*, 1937, pp. 22-23.
57. *Ibid.*
58. *Ibid.*, pp. 23-24.
59. *Ibid.*, 1940, pp. 54-55.
60. *Ibid.*, 1939, p. 168.
61. *Ibid.*, pp. 168-169.
62. *Ibid.*, 1940, p. 56.
63. *Ibid.*
64. *Ibid.*
65. *Ibid.*, p. 58.
66. *Ibid.*, p. 63.
67. *Ibid.*, p. 59.
68. *Ibid.*, p. 64.

69. *Ibid.*, 1937, p. 36.
70. *Ibid.*
71. *Ibid.*, pp. 37-38.
72. *Ibid.*, pp. 38-40.
73. *Ibid.*
74. *Ibid.*
75. *Ibid.*, p. 41.
76. *Ibid.*, p. 44.
77. *Ibid.*
78. *Ibid.*, p. 19.
79. *Ibid.*
80. In the chapter, "The Kingdom Comes With Power," in *The Choice Before Us* (1937), Stanley Jones gives in-depth treatment to the Kingdom of God -- embodied in the early Christian community -- "in miniature" as detailed in the fourth chapter of the book of Acts. He found that this account gave

> ...the true nature of a Christian society because at this place all the forces of the Christian dynamic had come into play: the teachings and example of Jesus, His death and resurrection and the coming of the Holy Spirit -- these constituted the Christian dynamic and were in operation producing new individuals and a new society. We therefore cannot see the true nature of a Christian Society until after Pentecost. But here we do. (pp. 52-53).

He then proceeds to break up this experimental Christian society as recorded in Acts 4:32-35 into its "constituent elements" to determine whether it provides an "ultimate order" affording "light and guidance in this confused world.." (p. 53). He identifies the Kingdom "elements" as being

> ...unity, profound and comprehensive...[and] not merely spiritual [but including] the economic and social; the basis of economic distribution was to each according to his need; the community life was fostered but the family and the individual were both preserved and heightened; the individual had found a great happiness because he had found a single-heartedness, life was reduced to inner simplicity; this new Society was God-centered and hence had meaning and ultimate worth; it commended itself to the people because it had become a classless society of brothers, and God worked in its behalf by adding the changed to their number, thus giving this new Society a basis for sustenance upon changed human nature. (p. 74).

Of course, it hardly needs to be said that Stanley Jones unpacks and examines these constituent elements in a very instructive and satisfactory way which we cannot replicate in these pages except in the most cursory, elementary sense. Stanley Jones better than anyone detected that this Society (Kingdom-of-God-in-miniature) glimpsed in Acts exhibited "one series of ultimates after another" and after careful scrutiny showed nothing that was "local, .. temporary, but always ... that which is ultimate and therefore abiding." He concludes that this Society "...had the germs of a new world in it. We must rediscover it and apply it fully to human living. It is the hope of the world -- the only hope that I can see." (pp. 74-75).

81. *Ibid.*, 1937, p. 65.
82. *Ibid.*
83. *Ibid.*
84. *Ibid.*
85. *Ibid.*, pp. 65-66.
86. *Ibid.*, p. 29.
87. *Ibid.*
88. *Ibid.*, pp. 29-30.
89. *Ibid.*, p. 40.
90. *Ibid.*
91. *Ibid.*, pp. 40-41.
92. The Kingdom "*was* prepared" from the foundation of the world -- "built into its very structure, the method of its working, the laws of its being. It is its life and the world cannot live apart from it or against it. When it tries to do so it perishes." (Jones, 1940, p. 59).
93. *Ibid.*, 1931, p. 312.
94. *Ibid.*, 1940, p. 63.
95. *Ibid.*, pp. 62-63.
96. *Ibid.*, p. 63.
97. *Ibid.*
98. *Ibid.*, p. 65.
99. *Ibid.*
100. *Ibid.*, p. 66.
101. *Ibid.*
102. *Ibid.*
103. *Ibid.*
104. *Ibid.*
105. *Ibid.*, p. 59.
106. *Ibid.*
107. *Ibid.*, p. 60.
108. *Ibid.*
109. *Ibid.*
110. *Ibid.*, p. 61.
111. *Ibid.*, pp. 60-61.

112. *Ibid.*, p. 58.
113. *Ibid.*, p. 184, 185.
114. *Ibid.* , p. 58.
115. *Ibid.*, p. 59.
116. *Ibid.*, p. 63.
117. *Ibid.*, p. 59.
118. *Ibid.*, p. 183.
119. *Ibid.*, pp. 183-184.
120. *Ibid.*, p. 185.
121. *Ibid.*, p. 58.
122. *Ibid.*
123. *Ibid.*
124. *Ibid.*, pp. 58-59.
125. *Ibid.*, pp. 56-57.

Chapter 7

The Disgraceful Disunity of the Church: Root Problem, Critique of the Present Context, Origin of the Rift Between Our Two Factions

Preoccupation with the Peripheral: Where the Church Has Blown It

Early in February of this year, while staying in the Asbury College guesthouse in order to use the very excellent library resources at Asbury Theological Seminary, my husband and I attended a Wednesday evening student-led prayer meeting in the campus auditorium. The President of Asbury College, Dr. Dennis Kinlaw, spoke on our need to know Christ. (Philippians 3:10). I recall now only the gist of Dr. Kinlaw's exhortation. What struck me from that experience was Dr. Kinlaw's opening remarks. It seems he had just returned from one of those meetings of a goodly number of everybodies who are anybodies among the evangelical leadership. Whatever occasioned the meeting, the sober sticking point for Dr. Kinlaw was the emergence of what he termed "four concerns to evangelicals": 1) "the increase of pluralism," 2) "disintegration of the evangelical core," 3) "separation of faith and life," and 4) "biblical illiteracy."

While I can appreciate the consternation which these admittedly serious concerns cause not only the evangelical guardians of the faith but others as well, and while it may smack of "cheap shot" tactics to latch onto this sensitive quartet of legitimate ills to launch an expose of where the Church has for the most part "blown it," nevertheless, these isssues are mere symptoms of a deeper, broader malady plaguing the Church. In other words the concerns cited by Dr. Kinlaw -- as exasperating and exacerbating as they are -- are peripheral not central. They point to the real root problem in the larger Church and, indeed, arise from it.

Moreover, these worrisome signs which have the evangelicals "all shook up" serve to shore up our emphasis on the fact that until and unless the Kingdom of God is recovered and we allow ourselves personally and corporately to be gripped by it, pledging total allegiance to it, we face continual demoralizing dissolution, enervating convulsions of ineffectiveness, clashes within (as among the conservative pentecostal-charismatic and liberal social justice factions) and crashes from events without, viz., adverse social pressures and world shattering events. Even the present fantastic burgeoning worldwide stemming from the evangelization of the pentecostal-charismatic wing of the Church will not hold unless that which is off-center, self-seeking, tending toward competitiveness, self-allegiance and self-satisfaction, within this wing is shifted to the only center that cannot be shaken, the Unshakable Kingdom. The warning has been long-standing yet unheeded so it must be sounded again:

> I am shakable, the society in which I live is shakable, the church to which I belong is shakable, the family in which I am rooted is shakable, the physical environment and the physical body which environs me [are] shakable, the very human life I live is shakable -- all are shakable, except one thing: the Kingdom of God. And only as I relate myself to that Kingdom by inner self-surrender and obedience do I find myself unshakable too.[1]

These four things that have captured the attention of the evangelical vanguard are indicative of those shocks of life in general and shocks of the faith in particular that inevitably come. Moreover, such shocks are bound to arise especially when too much reliance has been put on ways and resources which are part and parcel of whatever is less than or other than the Kingdom. In every instance where ultimate security or fullness of life is sought in the relative and shakable, in half-truths and lesser kingdoms, in partial and secondary relationships -- be they culture, class, economics, politics, church, denomination, family or race -- such shocks are met with acute dread, feverishness, collapse of confidence and courage (faith) and distressful aftereffects. Stanley Jones hits the nail on the head with these skillful words:

> ...every attempt by the individual and by society to seek for and to substitute anything in the place of the kingdom of God will end in dramatically swift or slow corrosive failure. It runs against the imponderables. Seek first the kingdom of God and all these things will be added. Seek something else first and all that you need will be subtracted.[2]

Admittedly it sounds like doubletalk or contradiction to allow that shakings (See and compare Hebrews 12:26ff.) are inevitable in one breath and then to imply in the next breath that they are precipitated more or less to the degree that Kingdom ways are sidestepped or not stringently adhered to. It is not simply either/or. The dual diagnosis pertains. But this one essential remains and it is here that the Church in all her multifarious stripes flounders in the crisis of her own making, in her self-inflicted centuries-old malady: the Church has not ceased refusing to receive the *whole* Kingdom that both redeems and reigns. The middle ground must go. This penetrating passage on the totalitarian, wholistic nature of the Kingdom undercuts the middle ground syndrome:

> ...God is not a half-god ruling over a half-realm, ruling over the personal but not over the social, or ruling over the social and not over the personal. .... He must be totally present and totally relevant or totally absent and hence totally irrelevant. .... And his kingdom must be totally present and totally relevant or totally nothing and hence totally irrelevant. .... He must be God of all or not God at all. And his kingdom must be a total kingdom or no kingdom.[3]

There can be no middle ground of partially receiving the Kingdom of God -- the doing of the will of God on earth as it is in heaven -- in "certain departments of life" and excluding it in others. No more restricting the Kingdom to the individual because it suits one's ecclesiastical or theological bent to preclude the social arrangements of the collective set-up from the sway of the Kingdom.[4] No more relegating the Kingdom solely to the future.[5]

The previous chapter observed the Kingdom in both its transcendent and immanent reality, its invading history and functioning within Time. (See Chapter 6). No more obfuscating the Kingdom by "binding it up with the Parousia -- the return of Christ."[6] Stanley Jones correctly discerns the exclusively futuristic stance that many in the Church have taken toward the Kingdom:

> Many who took the Kingdom took it in a modified form, as a personal spiritual refuge into which they could run and be safe now or as a place of reward in heaven; they didn't reject it; they reduced it. And in reducing it they rendered it innocuous *now*. It wasn't the Kingdom, God's total answer to man's total need. It wasn't God's total plan and program for life, all life, now, but a reward thrown in at the end.[7]

No more identifying the Absolute, totalitarian Kingdom of God with other relativistic kingdoms such as religion, socialism, capitalism, communism, Church, denomination or movement. The Kingdom of God expounded and exposed by Jesus -- exposed because he embodied it -- does not allow for these other kingdoms even to "color" the Kingdom. Stanley Jones offers this convincing conclusion on this very point:

> The kingdom of God may gather up into itself anything good in each of these, but in itself it is more than and other than any or all of these. It is unique in quality and quantity and goal and scope and objective. It is the most radical proposal ever proposed to the mind and allegiance of man. This is radicalism. .... And this is conservatism. It gathers up everything good in any system of thought and every religion anywhere, fulfills the good, cleanses the evil, and goes beyond anything ever thought or dreamed anywhere. This is the desire of the ages -- if men only knew it. All life, rational and subrational, is on tiptoe of expectancy for the kingdom of God, if man only knew it.[8]

In essence, the Kingdom of God both assimilates and eliminates while fulfilling and transforming continually to the glory of God.

If the preceding chapter on the Kingdom had the gargantuan, yet invigorating, task of presenting that unfathomable, all-encompassing Master-conception-plan-purpose-will, which Stanley Jones says, "gathers everything up into itself and gives it redemption, coherence, purpose, [and] goal,"[9] it is left to this chapter to undertake a less exhilarating expose. While muck raking is doubtless a too drastic and inappropriate term to describe the job to be done here, focusing on the shortcomings of the Church is, to say the least, an unappealling chore. The origin and evidence of the disunity of the Church coupled with the fact that this disunity impinges on and accounts for the present context of our two disagreeable parties pose a plateful of unpleasantness if for no other reason than that complete essays and entire books have done to death the ills, warts, blemishes, and/or problems of the Church -- and from every possible angle!

Apart from our critical opening salvo blasting the splintered Church for perpetually balking at total surrender to, hindering the realization of, and otherwise refusing and reducing the Kingdom-of-God revolution, where are we? Have we succumbed to the lust to engage in church-bashing by these preliminary, preemptive first strikes? We don't think so. We don't believe it is presumptuous to call ourselves as Christians to task for continuing to isolate the spiritual from the economic and material, to fail to be "spiritual in larger terms" by not using and directing "the material and economic toward spiritual ends."[10] The isolation of the spiritual should be a thing of the past,[11] but it isn't. It's a smugness that persists today to the blame and shame of the Church. Nor do we believe it overweening and hypercritical to denounce the Church for drawing a "line between the personal and the social and attempt[ing] to spiritualize the individual apart from his social relationships."[12] By apparently settling for an anti-Kingdom smugness that makes the personal "the special province of religion" thereby impoverishing both the personal and the social,[13] the Church continues to miss the mark and frustrate Kingdom goals.

The Dreaded 'C' Word: Compartmentalization

Compartmentalism is anathema to the Kingdom, yet the Church has covered up and condoned this superating sore which refuses to stay covered up and not surprisingly crops up on the evangelicals' "list of four" as "separation of faith and life." Stanley Jones identifies yet another sin of smugness or "fissiparous attitude"[14] underlying the life of the Christian Church which further attests to the confusion, breakdown, indifference, fear and hostility within and among the various faith departments:

> .the smugness of the devotional. We thought the devotional life was a thing apart and could be cultivated apart. Prayer was a personal communion with a personal loving God.[15] But we have found that God is not in the place we thought He was, namely, in the apart. He is bound up with life -- He is in its struggles, its pains, yes, in its very

> sins and failures, and suffers in them. You cannot, therefore, extract the devotional from the meeting of the very problems and pains and sins with which God is inextricably bound up. The sound of the tramp of the weary feet of the unemployed seeking for employment invades our sanctuaries of devotion, and we know now if we are to find God, we must find Him in the solution of these problems. For God is in them. Devotions to God and devotion to the needs of our brethren now become one. But religion is not geared into that thought. It is not at home with it. Such ideas belong to the radicals instead of the regulars. But the realization that the old compartmentalism is breaking down between devotions to God and devotion to man is slowly dawning.[16]

The slow dawning of the breakdown of old compartmentalisms, including the old chestnut of piety versus politics or faith shut off from life or orthodoxy over against orthopraxy, is slow indeed. Decades after Stanley Jones announced the creeping certain demise of the devotional life as "a thing apart," the Church still clings to the irreligion and perversion which ensue when personal private intimacy with God -- or even anointed corporate celebrations of genuine heartfelt high praise and worship -- is kept from being linked with the worship of God which springs from meaningful social engagement, doing service to and seeking justice for one's fellows especially the poor and so-called marginalized. This observation by Stanley Jones which is akin in tone and acuity to Old Testament prophets and Jesus' Kingdom teaching is not without sting: "For there is more of God in justice toward man than there is in gestures before God without that justice. (See James, especially 1:27, 2:5-8; 2:14-17). Many religious structures will have to come down that real religion may live."[17]

Unfortunately, we have not always paid attention to the glaring examples of hypocrisy that dot the Church's history line. Consequently, we tend to pride ourselves on adherence to a gospel that is pre-Christian and sub-Christian. These two examples from *The Christ of the Mount* zoom in on how many have not gotten beyond the spirit and ethic of the Old Testament:

> The Crusaders sang, "Fairest Lord Jesus, ruler of all nature," and then in his gentle name waded through blood in the streets of Jerusalem and praised him as they dashed out the brains of little children. Jesus was the rule of all nature, but certainly not of their natures. Sir John Browning wrote the sublime hymn, "In the Cross of Christ I Glory," and then went to China, where he sought to add to the commercial glory

of his nation by promoting the opium traffic. As Christ was tortured with the agonies of the opium victims and abased in the unjust profit accruing therefrom, how could he hear any praise in the hymn?[18]

Perhaps an updated example to parallel these rather dated cases might be detected in the case of Joe and Josephine Christian, who sing sweetly on Sunday, "Bless the Beasts and the Children" and on Tuesday pull the lever that returns to office mean-spirited representatives whose voting records predictably axe supplemental feeding programs such as WIC (Women, Infants and Children) and other time-proven, effective, safety-netted programs without which millions of children are doomed to slow agonizing deaths in poverty conditions.

To sum up: the foregoing discussion has explicitly cited the broad, albeit very serious, allegation against the Church for losing the gospel of the Kingdom of God and has zeroed in on the more specific proneness of the Church to compartmentalize. Consequently the door now swings wide open to expose once more the hesitations, half-denials, partial allegiances, faulty preconceptions, strengths and weaknesses of our two branches.

Pharisaical Preferences and a Pictorial Parody: 'Liberal SJAs, Look Out!'

Stanley Jones recounts the predilection of the Pharisees in thought and action to pick and choose certain religious niceties and moral requirements that more or less suited them and to eliminate the rest.[19] With typical pharisaical assiduousness the religious establishment of Jesus' day didn't actually reject all religious or ethical demands -- to do so would be sacrilege -- they simply "'passed by' ... and slurred them over and emphasized what was emphatic in their own inner loyalty. They built up a system of religion which left them complacent and comforted, because neatly compartmentalized."[20]

Lest we mistakenly think that this pahrisaical predilection is not alive and well today, let us imagine, for the sake of emphasis and, dare I say, the secret delight of the diehard conservative pentecostal-charismatic crowd, this deliberately, hopelessly stereotyped scenario.

Picture, if you will, our liberal social justice brethren (Translate: *contingent of left-wing, radical bleeding-heart, decadent, unpatriotic dissidents, humanistic malcontents, feminists and weirdos*) plunging headlong into the snarly briar patch of peace, social and economic justice issues (Translate: *the socialists' hidden political agenda*) by conducting a peaceful march (Translate: *conspiracy to attract already-biased-in-their-favor media attention while simultaneously provoking overreaction and violence from misunderstood over-worked, underpaid, scapegoated police officers*) down a greenbelt corridor stretching between a seated somber Lincolnesque saviour and, what looks like to everybody, an Indian-capped dome of democracy, but which, in fact, is a statue of freedom with an eagle on her head.

As they march in solidarity, shoulder to shoulder, hear them loudly chant grand stirring slogans (Translate: *anti-military establishment, anti-motherhood, anti-capitalism, anti-apple pie hogwash*) borne out of their having suffered the sticky consequences in sinister jails and having encountered the inevitable backlash of civil disobedience (Translate: *Law and Order violators deserve everything that's coming to them 'cause they should know better than to rock the boat and flaunt the system.*).

Having researched ad nauseum legislative minutiae, issued countless issue and position papers, bombarded public officials, high and low, with tons of letters with all the fervor and wily technique known to sweeping grassroots organizational ingenuity, these stalwarts of peace and justice (Translate: *unregenerate intellectualizing eggheads and communistic sympathizers*) are not entirely devoid of the transcendent impulse. Their careful nonjudgmental brainstorming and planning call for the kind of public demonstration (Translate: *jog-for-justice, hike-for-the-homeless, picnic-for-peaceniks or similar trite gimmickry*) that culminates in a solemn worship service in a gothic church or soup kitchen, with such celebrative communal observance sufficiently litanized and laced with the juciest social justice imperatives and prophetic bombasts from Isaiah, Micah, Gandhi, Martin Luther King, Jr., Eisenhower -- as a token tip to the few enlightened Republicans in their number -- and Dorothy Day (Translate: *dead ritual, deader religionists and religion; or 'What do you expect from constipated un-Spirit-filled, non-tongue-talking Main liners?'*).

For all the exaggerated satire, irony, and blatant irreverence in the above parody, it is not hard to detect inklings of truth and grounds for the legitimate charge of pharisaical predisposition endemic in *both* parties, conservative pentecostal-charismatic and social justice liberals alike. Liberal social justice adherents have tended to factor out the individual and the personal, the born-again experience (need for conversion,[21] repentance, confession -- all that the blood of Jesus the

Christ avails), the Person and explosive power of the Holy Spirit, miracles, signs and wonders, prayers of intercession, supplication, petition and intense spiritual warfare as preparatory to and decisive for any frontal assault on societal ills and injustices.

Let's face it. This particular wing of the Church has been running scared of the whole panoply of Pentecost, what to them is hocus-pocus pow-wow. Suffice it to say the liberal social justice advocates have given serious, dutiful heed to the heart cry of God for justice and social redemption. Moreover, they've been intentional about applying and embodying Kingdom laws and patterns in the social arena but only in their own limited, unreliable, collapsable strength, capacity and human resources apart from the Holy Spirit who is the "applied edge of redemption"[22] according to Stanley Jones. They've understood with theological acumen that back of Pentecost is the ethic, the moral backing of the Sermon on the Mount. In large measure their motivating passion has been enlarged as they've grasped that the Sermon on the Mount is not "unbelievably impossible [and] an absurdity"[23] as many in the Christian Church have supposed. They've not regarded the ethical side of Christianity as unworkable,[24] realizing to do so would be to render the redemptive side worthless.[25] They have not "emasculated and explained away" the Gospel at this crucial point.[26] But they have rather fallen down at the point of receiving "divine reinforcement" -- Pentecost -- emphasizing instead the dictum of their own exclusive pharisaical predilection that the power manifested at Pentecost is spiritual "pow-wow." So they opt instead to "rescue" the ethical backing of Pentecost, i. e., the Sermon on the Mount. On the contrary, they didn't rescue it, they divorced it, because what they didn't understand they were bound to fear.

Also to their credit the liberal social justice branch of the Church, apprehending better than others that Jesus' announcement of the new order and His instruction to pray for the Kingdom to come and come on earth as it is in heaven, realized that "the earth was not to be deserted and destroyed, but to be delivered and dedicated, the scene of the Kingdom of God."[27] In recognizing that the earth therefore "has a goal and destiny and its goal is to be added back to heaven from which it fell," the liberal social justice contingent has spearheaded the Church's advocacy for environmental protectionism and uncompromising stewardship in perfecting and co-creating the earth. Stanley Jones' interpretation of John's vision in Revelation is apropos: "'I saw a new heaven and a new earth' -- heaven and earth were to be wedded and both were to be new. That puts faith and hope and optimism at the heart of our dealing with this material world. It has a future."[28] Even if they have from time to time locked too firmly into the "material world" and have been wayward in their tilt toward immanence and a restricting concern for redemption apart from the vertical[29] and spiritual, the liberal social justice side has appreciated the doctrine of creation and reconciliation and restoration of the earth. In a polluting, polluted and rapacious world, commitment to renewal and regeneration of the earth is no small contribution to Kingdom goals and purposes.

Before leaving this condensed foray into certain selective flaws and good features of the liberals, we feel the need to stress this important idea that the material world has a destiny. Once again Stanley Jones serves as theological mentor in this excerpted discourse on the significance of the Word of God become flesh. Flesh, he says, stands for the whole material universe.

> This means that the Divine assumes a material body, not as a temporary garment put on and off at will. The word 'dwelt among us' could be translated 'tabernacled among us,' a permanent dwelling. This means that the material is not only going to be used for the purpose of the redemption of the spiritual being called man, but the whole person, his body included, and the whole material universe, are going to be redeemed. The material is just as much the subject of redemption as the spiritual. This plants the faith of Jesus squarely in the midst of human relationships -- nothing is alien to it except sin and evil . Anything that concerns life concerns the faith of Jesus, for He is Life and, therefore, includes everything comprehended under the term Life. The fact is that the Christian faith is the most materialistic of religions, the only one that really takes the material seriously. It starts out by saying that when God created the material universe, He 'saw it was good' -- the material was God-made and God-approved.[30]

Pharisaical Preferences and Another Pictorial Parody: 'Conservative P/Cs, Watch It!'

As they say, one good rollicking parody deserves another. This time for the amusement of the social-justice liberals, we turn the fair-play spotlight on the pentecostal/charismatic conservatives. Picture once more, if you will, the *big*, nay, *jumbo* Bible-toting faithful in their electrifying bouffanted-moussed-spritzered hairdos, grinning like horses eating sawbriars, glad handing and bestowing super syrupy 'God bless you!' and 'Praise the Lord!' greetings right and left, streaming up high speed escalators, secured at bottom and top by elderly yellow-jacketed trouble-shooting ushers, on into the steep-seater, triple-tiered convention hall engulfed by a throbbing tantalizing din of one good amplified orchestra-blaring, foot-stomping, toe-tapping, hand-clapping, off-the-wall praise chorus after another and the let 'er rip bless me meeting is under way. (Translate: *The crazy theologically thin fanatics have hit town big time.*).

What follows at this week-long, unprecedented, interdenominational, prayer-soaked, Holy Spirit-orchestrated, months-in-the-making, renewal conference on world evangelism is a plethora of power-packed prophecies, preaching services and marathon seminars on soul-winning, a surge of spontaneous worship and praise and healings and deliverances, a heap of hall-way mini-miracles as humble-hearted folks hold hands and intercede in the sweetly strange glossal languages of the Spirit for one another's personal battles and bondages, the tearing down through strong spiritual warfare of satanic strongholds over entire cities, and strategic street ministry and witnessing by Bible Bowl-seasoned kids and turned-on-youth. All this is topped off with a bit of innocent flag-waving and two-way congratulatory messages exchanged between White House and conventioneers relative to the "miracle" victory in the Persian Gulf. (Translate: *The divisive, tongue-talking, rabidly patriotic, status-quo supporting, swing-into-town-stuff-a-religious-tract-into-the-torn-pockets-of-the-down-and-out-homeless-and-bid-Godspeed, prosperity-parleying, faith-will-fix-it-mouthing, my-brand-of-Christianity's-right-and-yours-ain't, get-government-off-our-backs-tax-rebelling-take-our-kids-out-of-the-humanistic-ridden-public-schools-and-let-the-public-schools-be-damned, Charismatic-two-steppin', militaristic Moral Majority maniacs are bound to mess up the Church and society and set enlightened, egalitarian, pluralistic democracy back to the time before the dinosaurs.*)

In many ways the conservative pentecostal-charismatic branch has "earned" its way to center-stage stardom amid growing admiration and respect (if somewhat begrudgingly bestowed by those no longer in the ascendancy) within Christianity. As no group before, they have received and responded to the stirrings of the Holy Spirit and welcomed the manifestations of His powerful supernatural gifts and deeds. In their letter dated May 2, 1990, Oral Roberts University graduates Billy Joe and Sharon Daugherty, co-founders/pastors of the 9,000-plus member Victory Christian Center in Tulsa, Oklahoma, wrote:

Entire denominations missed out on great blessings from God because they did not know that the Charismatic movement was sent to bless and enrich churches. History is filled with incidents of people moving in God's time to do great things, such as Esther speaking to the King and saving her people, the Jews. To know the times and seasons is to have God's wisdom. It is the Spirit of God that imparts this understanding to us.

As we meditate on God's Word, hear anointed preaching/teaching and listen to God in prayer we will receive revelation of His timing.

In January, 1983 Pastor Billy Joe says that the Lord spoke to him that "'Revival is coming to North America.'" In a letter to ministry partners dated August 28, 1989, Pastor Daugherty writes that he received instruction from the Lord to "sound an alarm to get people ready for it." In commenting on the prerequisites for revival, to "receive the move of God's Spirit [and] cause the harvest to come," Pastor Daugherty says, "Signs, wonders and miracles will accompany the coming revival. Those who reject and fight the supernatural demonstration of the Holy Spirit will see the river change its course and leave them dried up in dead ritualism. Wherever the Word of God is proclaimed with power, God will confirm it with signs following."

Without question the pentecostal-charismatic current within the wider conservative evangelical stream of the Church, by hungering for, recognizing, and cooperating with the Holy Spirit and His move across this historically most recent stage of Pentecostal visitation, has received enormous benefits from what Stanley Jones calls "divine reinforcement."[31] Astonishing spiritual revitalization of individuals and groups, enlivening transformations in praise and worship, an unprecedented outbreak of the miraculous running the every-area-of-life gamut, unparalleled gains in membership in both new converts as well as in disenchanted or wayward believers, and a most impressive and effective impact on certain parts of society at home and abroad via a wide array of ministry outreach and mission programs are among the very real benefits that have overtaken this group in the receptivity to the Person and power of the Holy Spirit.

Generally speaking, in contrast to the liberal faction, this branch of Christianity is to be congratulated for refusing to shun the Holy Spirit. They have rightly opted for the "absolute necessity" and that which only Pentecost provides and without which we "cannot be Christian in any vital sense."[32]

So far so good. But that's precisely the rub. Infected with the same pharisaical passion for selectivity vis-a-vis Kingdom requirements as the liberals, the conservative pentecostal-charismatics have not gone far enough. They are content with stopping short of the full Gospel, of giving full rein to that "applied edge of redemption" that would cut through the insidious accretions of social, political and economic institutional life, exposing and challenging the unjust underpinning of unholy and injurious policies and decision-making practices. In short, they tend to shy away from what would be dangerous confrontation -- as prescribed in the Sermon on the Mount -- with every "underlying conception on which modern society is built."[33]

If the liberals have "toned down and made 'safe'"[34] the Way of Pentecost as *the* way of empowerment for living the individual Christian life and tapping into the supernatural manifestations of the Holy Spirit for witnessing and edification, the conservative pentecostal-charismatics have done the same number on the larger ethical demands of the Kingdom for radical transformation and realignment toward the New World Order with respect to the social dimension.

Rather than striking at the whole selfish competitive motif so rampant in modern economic life and demanding that "men cooperate in love or perish in strife,"[35] the conservative pentecostal-charismatics have endorsed and made sacrosanct the cut-throat economic system and have indulged and exuded in political economic laissez-faire triumphalisms. Especially have they embraced it when it is perceived as having "worked" for them despite the recognized taint deriving from the fact that it is part and parcel of the "world's system." When they haven't altogether endorsed or embraced it, they have chosen to castigate and shun it, together with the *real* culprit, *the* government. They tend to see the whole range of societal institutional life (economics, education, politics and culture) as not only unworkable but also hopelessly doomed to eventual chaos and devastation, unredeemed and unredeemable, because it is controlled and manipulated by "the devil's crowd." Then the assumed attitude is one of hands-off detachment. Scriptural admonition and justification such as "Come out from among them and be separate." and "The wealth of the sinner is laid up for the just." become plausible shibboleths for an end-time scenario which promises increased evil and rampant "signs" of disaster and turmoil in every conceivable quarter and corner. This view is not without a measure of truth. But it is also not without its prejudicial distortions. For example, there is immense comfort for all believers in Psalm 46 which acknowledges God as "refuge and strength and ever-present help in trouble." (NIV).

This much-loved psalm conveys deep, unshakable conviction that God is the Lord Almighty, possessing absolute power to save and deliver even in the midst of staggering earthly desolation and cataclysm.

It is good to learn fearlessness from this psalm which says, "Therefore we will not fear, though the earth give way and the mountains fall into the heart of the sea, though its waters roar and foam and the mountains quake with their surging." (See verses 2-3NIV). But it is the height of spiritual selfishness to invoke its providential tenor, along with other selected scripture passages, as has been the case within the charismatic-pentecostal circles to teach that even if the world's economic system collaspes and "the devil's crowd" suffers complete ruination "by crumbling into the sea," [verse 3bKJV] bless God, such a plague of economic woe won't come near me. There's something here which is alien to the Christ Spirit which "loved the world [including those in spiritual blindness, i.e., "the devil's crowd"] so much..." It's another spirit which seems akin to the old backyard fall-out shelter, built for me and mine, mentality of the 50s.

Like it or not, admit it or not, it is not fanciful to suggest that in their ideological rush to approve wholesale dismantling of (to their minds) odious big government budgets and programs, the conservative pentecostal-charismatics have rather belatedly begun to "minister to" the estimated 2,000,000 and growing numbers of homeless persons whom they, in effect, condemned to the streets by their vote to decimate the very programs and budgets designed to prevent hunger and homelessness!

Nor is it beyond the mark to suggest that this group has been asleep when it comes to a brand of patriotism that sees no wrong or danger in militarization. Blind patriotism which condones lying and deception by government officials, aides and advisors -- not to mention making heroes out of those who have admitted to lying before Congressional committees -- has mislaid the Truth of the Way which holds that no convenient, artificial separation of means and ends is allowed because the end always contains the means. To support lies (misinformation, disinformation and cover-up) and deceit as an acceptable means, for example, of "protecting the national interest" secures nothing. Would Jesus allow lying, pretense, perversion as a way to attain any good aim? Hardly. To rationalize and suppose otherwise is pure self-deception and gross sin. To try to skirt the standard by bifurcating morality into private and public sectors is iniquitous and will not work because the Kingdom won't back it. Stanley Jones clearly shows the impossibility of baptizing patriotism:

> Patriotism is a false god. It is forbidden to the true Christian to blindly embrace patriotism and attendant military might. Because it carries within it the corrupting seed, the betraying tendency to substitute moral and spiritual battlefields for real ones. By moral confusion, it seduces believers away from total allegiance to Christ who embodies the Kingdom of God. He forgets, blocks out, turns his back on the highest spiritual reality, the Truth that says overcome evil with good, hate by love and the world by a cross of suffering for the world.[36]

Christians of whatever stripe -- left, right or center -- for the sake of preserving their political predispositions are skating over the dangerous icy dual sins of blasphemy and dehumanization when they indulge or let stand without comment vulgarizations and warlike rhetoric such as "kick ass." Such assertive tough talk from the mouths of politicians, presidents or generals or ordinary citizens looses a demonic spiritual force that goes byond mere patriotic passion and insinuates a hideous demeaning devil that is strictly forbidden in and diametrically opposed to the Gospel of Jesus Christ. Nothing is more sacred to God than human personality. To view even so-called enemies as less than human, just so much "ass to kick around" is to trample the judgment of God -- and the unfathomable love, forgiveness, reconciliation which is the Cross -- under one's feet. Those who use such vulgar expressions betray a Nazi mentality that implies that "any ass" different from our own is fair game for kicking.

The propensity of this group of Christians, whom we have labeled conserative pentecostal-charismatics, to insulate their cultural prejudices and political biases in a shroud of Biblical half-truths and selected ethical interpretation is seen in their capitulation to war. As we've already shown Christ and His Kingdom are unalterably opposed to war.[37] To engage in warfare one has to hate. Hatred is forbidden to the Christian. Any erroneous viewpoint sanctioning war even as a "last resort" is at cross purposes with the Kingdom of God.

The Need To Be Against

In August of 1988, while attending a "Word Explosion!" at Victory Christian Center in Tulsa, we had the privilege of hearing Dr.

Benson Idahosa of Nigeria preach powerfully on the demand for those who have the Spirit of Christ to cast out devils, to be against everything that God in Christ Jesus is against or everything that is unclean. (See Matthew 10:1). Bishop Idahosa could very well have been the sanctified counterpart to General Patton as he aroused and rallied the "troops" (believers) into battle with his crescendo-building commands: "Poverty is not clean. Be against it. Dying is not from God. It is unclean. Be against it. Sickness is not from God. It is unclean. Be against it." And so on. He was saying in essence, "Be against anything that is unlike God." We believe it would not have violated his text to include the unwavering command to be against war and economic exploitation, selfishness, and competitiveness.[38] Jesus really is against war and we do need to be against it. War is inherently wrong and anti-Christ. Shouldn't we be against and resist with every Holy Spirit-stimulated fiber of our being war? War, says Stanley Jones, cannot be "softened" or "naturalized;" it has be to "eliminated."[39] The problem is that Christians, with this group of the Church in the lead, have emasculated and explained away the Kingdom pattern at this point and have furthered the naturalization and softening of war to the point of slipping into calling good evil and evil good.

Bishop Idahosa was right in portraying God as loving the world so much that he sent His Son into the enemy's camp, to a cross to defeat evil, to win the real war, and to win us who were doomed back to Himself. But he was remiss in not calling believers to renounce and be against war.

We would be remiss to omit this profound observation by Stanley Jones which is pertinent to our contention that *all* Christians must "be against" whatever opposes the very center and substance of the Kingdom:

> Obviously, if religion is to influence life, it cannot be embodied in personal attitudes alone. The principles and spirit of it must be embodied in the social order, for whatever is in the social order converts, in large measure, those under that order. If religion turns over the social, the economic, and the political to other ways of life, and hopes to influence the individual through personal contacts, it will be fighting a losing battle. The situation is loaded against its success. True, it will influence individuals here and there, and we must be grateful for that influence, but it makes religion the occasional and the marginal instead of the central formative fact in life. Shall we rescue individual slaves and leave untouched the slave traffic? Shall we pick

> up individual drunkards and leave untouched the liquor traffic? Shall we gather up the wounded in war and attend to them and leave the war system operative? Shall we pick up the derelicts of a ruthlessly competitive order and give them doles and handouts, or shall we put justice and the love of God into the order so that this shall be unnecessary? Obviously, we must do both, for evil can be in the individual will and it can be in the collective will. There is such a thing as an evil soul and there is such a thing as an evil system. If we do not undertake to cure evil in the social order, then religion becomes an ambulance corps in human life picking up the wounded instead of a banner leading the army.[40]

Sad to say, our conservative element has given precious little thought and attention to and examination and exposure of "impersonal causes of evil" or those things in society which make people sin. Such obstinate, inordinate and exclusive emphasis on the personal nature of sin resonates a hard-heartedness toward society and its marginalized and victimized which betrays the Christ-Spirit. After all, Jesus sat and continues to sit where we messed-up, broken mortals sit, and felt and continues to feel what we feel and yet still loves us, visits us, redeems us and ever offers to remove the yoke of bondage (both those personal and impersonal forces which are responsible for sin and misery and separation) and take the heavy burdens off our personal and corporate shoulders and to give us His rest. (See Matthew 11:28-30).

The Anti-Kingdom Triad

Again, we must expose the triad of anti-Kingdom attitudes which have the earmarkings of the conservative evangelical pentecostal-charismatic wing:

1. Convert enough individuals and change society for the better automatically.
2. The less controversial route of giving charity is preferable to doing justice where justice can be done.
3. Endorse existing governmental (administrative) policies and practices even when these are contrary to the Kingdom because those within the Executive Branch of Government know best and we shouldn't second guess their decisions and coure of action.

As to the first faulty hang-up our reply is that it does not necessarily follow that by changing individual wills you automatically alter the social order for the better.[41] Stanley Jones offers this wise counterargument: "[t]he social order is not made up of individuals now living -- it is made up of inherited attitudes, institutions, customs, laws, and these exist, in large measure, independently of the individual wills now living."[42] The changing of these individual wills does not of necessity change society unless "you organize those changed individual wills into social action on a wide-scale, frontal attack upon those corporate evils."[43]

If this pet conservative maxim were true then we must ask why it is that so many "deeply religious men" in South Africa are so "oblivious to this social evil" called apartheid? The answer is simple but troubling: their Christianity has always been interpreted and maintained in "very personal terms."[44] The observation is rightly stated:

> You could change every single person in the world today by an individual conversion, and unless you put the content of social change into that individual conversion your social order will remain exactly what it is. As Dr. Halford E. Luccock says, 'By sinking individual wells in your back yard you do not thereby have a city water system.' I repeat -- if the Kingdom of God is totalitarian, then it must take in the whole of life, and life includes both the social and the personal.[45]

Fiji is the classic recent case that comes to mind. Having achieved through evangelistic endeavor a Christian population in the 90-plus percentage range, very shortly after this milestone was attained and publicized in Christian magazines, there was a political takeover which definitely had a clamp-down effect on the island nation as a whole.[46]

It is terribly tempting to object to the second wrong notion with a touch of sarcasm. If charity is the sole pattern for social relationships derived from the Kingdom Way, then Haiti should be a virtual paradise. Sadly, this is not reality for the poorest country -- and the most populous -- in the western hemisphere. One can hardly come up with a better frontline recipient of longstanding, continual charity from every denominational group within the United States than Haiti. The kind of justice that Jesus was and is "passionately interested in" is a justice "that will mean a just distribution of what God intends for His children."[47] Stanley Jones leaves no doubt as to what Jesus meant when he added the term "and his justice" to the "Seek ye first" imperative:

> He added it for emphasis -- the Kingdom meant 'justice.' Now, 'justice' or 'judgment' had a very definite social content in the minds of His hearers, for the prophet has insisted: 'Sow justice for yourselves, and reap a harvest of God's love' (Hosea 10. 12, Moffatt); 'No more of your hymns for me! .... No, let justice well up like fresh water, let honesty roll in full tide' (Amos 5. 23, 24, Moffatt). With this content in their thinking they would know at once what Jesus meant by 'justice' -- it meant, not a legal justice, but right relations between man and man. But Jesus was putting into it a further very definite content: justice would be right relations between man and man *accodring to Kingdom-of-God standards.* Seek *that,* said Jesus and everything in the economic you need will be added unto you. We are not seeking that, and as a consequence these things are not being added to us. We are hungry amid plenty because we refuse to do justice. Charity? Yes, we are willing to give charity to the poor; in fact, we are willing to give them everything, except one thing -- justice.[48]

Finally, this third deception has been dealt with elsewhere. But it needs to be underscored that that religion which obliges itself to sanction the order that exists, to avoid criticism of political wrongdoing, and to naturalize and conform itself to political ideologies incompatible with the Christ Spirit betrays the prophetic word. To put it a bit differently: "The critic-from-within-the-establishment, the house prophet, will, if he stays inside when the crunch comes, be with Herod after all."[49]

For six years or more we have been in many wonderful charismatic services. We have heard a good many edifying "prophecies" come forth as the inspirational gift of prophecy was manifested. We have yet to hear one word of exception that would indicate a stance at odds with government policy relative to social-economic justice questions either at home or abroad, let alone a full-blown prophetic sermon in which the status quo political leadership is ever called into question on such issues, shown to be opposed to Kingdom justice and Christ's ways and consequently directly admonished and challenged to repentance and reform. This puzzles and greatly disturbs us. We simply don't understand.

Efficacies and Errors

In this chapter we have tried to take a probing look at the efficacies and errors of our two wings in order to come to terms with the sorry state of the fractured Church. We have seen that evidence for the present disharmonies abounds and cannot honestly be denied or ignored. We have suggested that compartmentalism and pharisaism, while sounding old hat, are really alive and well in the Church and as subtly and imperceptibly leavening as pump-up jogging shoes. By consciously or unconsciously opting for an incomplete ethic, half-truths, a partial Gospel and a scaled-down King and Kingdom; by failing to drag all intransigence and recalcitrance into the light of self-judgment to declare, "'My God, [we] have been guilty there.'";[50] by eclipsing the central attitude and invitation of Christ and His Kingdom to self-renunciation, to self-surrender, and to lose the lower life to gain the higher Life, our two separated parties keep the Church cracked apart and are guilty of what Oswald Chambers called the deadliest Pharisaism or "unconscious unreality."[51]

It has not been our aim merely to pick flaws. Believing, however, that a biting humor can help to attract and focus our attention long enough to coax us toward an initially scary look at the heuristic value of the "other" side and simultaneously at our own foibles, we have stooped to stereotype and parody. If our hard-hitting, spare-no-offender approach in this chapter has done anything it surely has made clear that the present context is totally unacceptable. In *A Church Truly Catholic*, Bishop James K. Mathews writes,

> For too long the disunity of the Church has been a scandal. .... Karl Barth observed long ago that a divided church is 'ontologically quite impossible; it is possible only as sin is possible.' The time has more than come to renounce our divisiveness as we would renounce sin; that God may heal our divisions.[52]

So be it. As we said earlier, the Church has blown it. But one thing remains before we seal off this chapter. If the Church itself is to blame for its own disunity, how and when did the sin of division occur? For the origin of disunity we turn to the New Testament and the book of Acts, with oversight from our Kingdom mentor Stanley Jones.

The Misstep

Do with it what you will, there is no greater betrayal of the Founder of the Faith than that found among the spiritual leaders in the early Church. In the case of the dispute over the neglect of the Greek widows in the daily distribution of food, the disciples were right in that they saw "that spirituality was a prerequisite and that it must function in this business of food distribution."[53] Their instructions were: "...seek out from among you seven men of good reputation, full of the Holy Sprit and wisdom, whom we may appoint over this business; but we will give ourselves continually to prayer and to the ministry of the word." (Acts 6:3-4TNKJV). But they were wrong and betrayed the character of Jesus when they said, "'It is not desirable that we should leave the word of God and serve tables.'" (verse 2TNKJV). In refusing to drop preaching the word to attend to meals and possibly necessary financial arrangements (Who said they had to stop preaching?), the disciples, as Stanley Jones says, missed their step...

> for here they made a distinction which has become a very disastrous one in Christian history. They were untrue to the Master who did not hesitate to 'attend to meals' for the multitudes in the wilderness, and who made of a last meal a sacrament which lives through the ages, and who after His resurrection prepared a morning meal for His hungry disciples by the lakeside after a night of toil.[54]

Also worth mentioning is the case where Jesus did not disdain getting involved in money matters relative to a very pressing tax deadline which apparently bore down on Jesus and at least one of his disciples. When the tax man accosted Peter in Capernuaum with the business of the temple tax which he alleged that Jesus owed, Peter, whose motive is unclear, quickly agreed that the tax would be paid. Discerning that Peter had been pressed in the matter by the officious tribute collectors, Jesus sent Peter down to the sea to catch the first fish to surface, extract the coin from its mouth and pay what was owing for the two of them. (See Matthew 17:24-27).

To return to the "misstep" and what is so pivotal about it, let us note this comment by Stanley Jones: "The apostles withdrew from that stream of the sacredness of all life and of all tasks in the Kingdom, and started a tendency to try to spiritualize life apart from the material."[55]

The sheer folly of driving a wedge between the interlocking spiritual and material aspects of life is a lesson not lost on Stanley Jones and should not be lost on us. The calamitous effect has been that by their ostensibly innocuous decision, the early apostles...

> made the clergy into a group apart, looked on as impractical visionaries, instead of the solid architects of a new order working their way through material relationships to the establishment of the Kingdom within those relationships. God did His best to break up that distinction, for He used Stephen as an evangelist far more than the apostles who thus separated themselves. [See Acts 6:8,10Moffatt].
>
> God did not accept the distinction the apostles were making, broke it down and used the table-servers in the area where the disciples were supposed to be specialists, namely, the spiritual, far more than the apostles themselves. They should have taken the hint. Philip, one of these table-servers, became 'Philip the evangelist,' God not allowing the distinction between evangelist and table server to remain. Paul took the hint and could say, 'You know yourselves how these hands of mine provided everything for my own needs and for my companions. I showed you how this was the way to work hard and succor the needy, remembering the words of the Lord Jesus, who said, "To give is happier than to get"' (Acts 20. 34, 35 Moffatt). [See II Thessalonians 3:7-10Moffatt]. Paul saw the principle of the unity of the so-called secular and sacred more than the other apostles. .... He stood for the lay side of things and was looked on as a layman -- and he was! But in doing so he was true to the genius and spirit of the gospel. For Christ was a layman and His movement was a lay movement, bringing the Kingdom down into the total life and making the total life sacred.[56]

What it all boils down to is this: the Church took a misstep and instigated the separation of life from life (the sacred or spiritual from the material or secular) thereby overturning the Kingdom of God challenge that "the whole of life come under one dominance, one sway."[57] *What the Holy Spirit did not endorse but has apparently "allowed" in order not to override our free moral agency has been the uncorrected legacy of the Church through the ages from which has sprung the sharp separation as outlined in our two opposing churches with their partial Kingdom emphases vying for a position of superiority, the one side over the other.*

This incident from Acts tells but part of the story. Stanley Jones supplys us with additional evidence that a pattern of division and usurpation of Kingdom inclusiveness and unifying economy by compartmentalism and a faulty view of the wholistic Gospel began early on setting the stage for the present chasm between the conservative pentecostal-charismatics and the liberal social justice faction. Stanely Jones writes,

> In the early Church there were really two communions. One was the communion of the Bread and Wine in which they communed with the crucified and risen Lord. The other was the communion with each other in the breaking of Bread, a rite which was known as the 'Agape,' or Love Feast. This Love Feast was a very serious thing and had a profound meaning which went to the very center of human relationships. The second communion grew out of the first communion -- as they were Brothers of the Bread so they extended this Brotherhood beyond the spiritual communion into an economic and social communion. As they were one at the place of the altar, they would be one at the place of the economic. The Brotherhood of the Bread was not confined to a momentary partaking of Bread in a sacred place, it would extend itself into a Brotherhood of the Bread in the ordinary partaking of bread for sustenance. 'They distributed according to each man's need' ... for, 'They had all things common.' It was a Brotherhood of the One Bread. They were united in the material. .... The material and spiritual were under a single dominance.
>
> They also belonged to the Brotherhood of the Blood. .... It was one Bread and one Blood and there were no limits or hesitations. Life was unified. It was the most magnificent conception ever presented to the mind of man. Had the Christian Church remained true to this, it would have transformed the world...
>
> But what did the Christian Church do? We kept the communion with Christ and dropped the communion with each other. The Agape dropped out and the Eucharist remained. Why? Apparently for the reason that we could compartmentalize life at this place -- we could commune with each other spiritually in a mystic communion at the altar, but there the communion would cease. We would co-operate at the place of the sacred Bread and compete at the place of the common bread. A wedge was driven straight into life -- the most disastrous wedge ever driven into the soul of humanity. The pulling out of that wedge must now be the chief business of the Christian Church.[58]

Not until we had read these and other remarkable, revelatory passages in Stanley Jones' books were we able to see when and how the Church began to go off-center. It was now clearer to us why and how various churches within the Church came to be at odds with each other over particular pet gospels and certain elements of the faith that should never have been debatable because they were and are parts of one process and should go hand in hand.[59] Yes, the Church is to blame becaue it let go the Kingdom emphasis, its patterns, attitudes, approaches and concomitantly reduced it, placed it beyond the border of this life, toned it down and made it safe or interpreted it in too narrow and small a way. In short, to put it curtly, the Church took the new sphere of living, the Kingdom of God -- that which Jesus Christ made central and fundamental[60] -- emasculated it, marginalized it. It broke apart and splintered itself in the process.

Is the divided Church, exemplified in the estrangement of our two wings, poor and needy enough, sick enough of its disgraceful disunity, willing enough to be criticized and corrected, open enough to the Holy Spirit to be led to repentance, renewal, and empowerment for obedience to the Kingdom -- its absoluteness, truth and discipline? *If* the answer from all concerned will be yes, we are willing to be confronted and reawakened and, at least, willing to be made willing to be receptive to recovering the Kingdom as the dynamic and "principle of unity amid differences,"[61] the **HOPE** may yet stir, scintillate, surprise and beckon us into the "new day"[62] beyond what we could ask or imagine.

Notes

1. Jones, 1949, p. 262.
2. *Ibid.*, 1972, p. 77.
3. *Ibid.*, pp. 14-15.
4. *Ibid.*, p. 75.
5. The emphasis on a future Kingdom with future implications that has most often been held by the Church has tended to overshadow and cancel out the Kingdom of God as present, as now with now implications. We recall that "Philip and Paul both preached 'the kingdom and the name of Jesus' as now issues." (*Ibid.*, p. 74).
6. *Ibid.*, p. 73.
7. *Ibid.*, p. 16.
8. *Ibid.*, pp. 26-27.
9. *Ibid.*, p. 75.
10. *Ibid.*, 1937, p. 10.
11. *Ibid.*
12. *Ibid.*
13. *Ibid.*
14. *Ibid.*, p. 13.

15. Of course prayer entails personal communion and intimacy with a loving God. The Holy Spirit desires nothing so much as companionship and utter closeness with each and every believer. Many fine books have been devoted to discovering and cultivating a personal relationship with the Holy Spirit which is absolutely indispensable to the spiritual adventure and formation of every single Christian. This aspect of the reality and truth of prayer is not in question. But there is more to the life of prayer and this more is the focal point in this context.

Stanley Jones offers this definition of prayer: "*Prayer is co-operation with God.* In prayer you align your desires, your will, your life to God. You and God become agreed on life desires, life purposes, life plans, and you work them out *together*." He also quotes another definition of prayer: "'To bring the whole of life into the presence of God for cleansing and decision.'" He goes on to elaborate:

> 'For cleansing and decision' -- prayer cleanses, it chastens our desires, realigns them so that you cannot tell where your desires end and God's desires begin. They are one. Since the desires are one, the decisions are one, and the power is one. You lay your impotence alongside of God's potence and lo, your impotence has merged into potence, yes, into omnipotence. When you learn how to pray, you learn how to live -- vitally, vibrantly, victoriously. (Jones, 1946, p. 197).

It would be time well invested to examine Stanley Jones' powerful teaching on prayer which looks at the unfolding meanings in the Lord's Prayer and deals with prayer as reality, receptivity, response, renewal, revision, relaxation, release, and rejoicing. He finishes up the section on prayer set forth in *The Way* by suggesting practical steps to take in establishing a real prayer life. (See pages 197-217, *The Way*).

16. *Ibid.*, pp. 11-12.

17. *Ibid.*, 1939, p. 66.

18. *Ibid.*, 1931, p. 117.

19. *Ibid.*, 1940, p. 164.

20. *Ibid.*, p. 165.

21. Stanley Jones references three steps in the transformation process called conversion:

> 1. *A new direction* -- 'except ye be converted.' .... Conversion is first of all a new direction, a reversal. But it is a turning *with* -- it is not turning around in general. It is a turning around specifically -- with Christ.
>
> 2. *A new spirit* -- 'and become as little children.' A fresh beginning, the spirit of a child possesses you, you are reduced to simplicity from

the complexities and complications of evil. ....

3. *A new sphere of living* -- 'enter into the kingdom of heaven.' You pass out of the sphere of the kingdom of self and enter the sphere of the Kingdom of God. You change worlds. Here in this new sphere of living you and God work out life *together*. You supply willingness and He supplies power. Life is no longer on the unit principle -- it is now a co-operative affair -- you and God in partnership, with God the senior partner and managing director. The lonely orphanced striving is gone, and now a sense of being together with One who has all the answers and all the resources for carrying out those answers takes possession of you. You feel you *belong* and belong to Adequacy. (Jones, 1951, p. 22).

22. *Ibid.*, 1972, p. 72.
23. *Ibid.*, 1931, p. 16.
24. Stanley Jones says,

So morality is not based on the will of God. It is based on the character of God. Everything God asks us to do -- he does. He is not a finger-post pointing the way. He is the loving shepherd saying, "Come follow me." So morality is not something imposed, but something exposed, something exposed out of the very character of God. ...[it] is not something verbal -- it is vital, out of life, God's life. (Jones, 1972, pp. 106-107).

The Sermon on the Mount encapsulates and authenticates this profound theological given.

25. *Ibid.*, 1931, p. 17.
26. *Ibid.*, p. 16.
27. *The Theology and Missiology of E. Stanley Jones*, p. 5.
28. *Ibid.*
29. Stanley Jones puts the need for vertical conversion in clear terms: "We feel our real life in the higher, in the Kingdom of God. .... Vertical conversion is that spiritual change wrought by Christ that lifts us from sin to goodness, from discord to harmony, for selfishenss to sacrifice, from ourselves to God and gives us a new sphere of living, the Kingdom of God." (*The Theology and Missiology of E. Stanley Jones*, p. 71.).
30. *Ibid.*, p. 5.
31. *Ibid.*, 1931, p. 18.
32. *Ibid.*
33. *Ibid.*, p. 19.
34. *Ibid.*, p. 18.
35. *Ibid.*, p. 19.

36. *Ibid.*, pp. 99-100.

37. Were the following quotation shared with the typical pentecostal-charismatic congregation one wonders how many would be shocked to hear such words for the very first time and whether the reaction would be one of conditioned disbelief and indifference or of genuine dis-ease and dismay thereby triggering a whole new thought and outlook:

> For the first three centuries of the Christian Church no Christian ever went to war and no soldier stayed in the army after he became a Christian. The soul of Christianity was unified at the place of the use of armed force -- it was judged incompatible with the Christian way of life. Then with the conversion of Constantine no one except a Christian could get into the army. There Christianity brought into its inmost soul an incompatibility and divided itself against itself. This foreign substance brought into the body of Christianity has been a festering place through the ages. We have tried to naturalize war in the body of Christianity by softening it and trying to make it humane. But it cannot be done. (Jones, 1940, p. 169).

38. The economic is another realm in which the Church has inwardly divided itself and set itself at odds with the Kingdom. This tremendous reflection powerfully documents the disastrous results of Christianity's willful disobedience by embracing the "incompatible element of selfish ruthless, economic competition":

> Competitive capitalism and Christianity tried to come to a working alliance -- Christianity would take over the severely spiritual portions of life and leave the economic and hence the social political relations to a selfish struggle for profit. The man of business became two men: on Sunday a man of co-operation and love and on Monday a man of competition and selfish accumulation. He was not a hypocrite -- far from it. He was a victim of a division which Christianity took within itself. He tried to be two men at one and the same time -- a Christian man with love and mutual aid as the driving forces of his life, and an economic man with selfishness and mutual elimination as the driving forces of his life. The awakened modern Christian is a very unhappy man, for he knows that he is a house divided against itself. (Jones, 1940, p. 170).

39. *Ibid.*, 1940, p. 169.
40. *Ibid.*, 1937, pp. 168-169.
41. *Ibid.*, p. 170.
42. *Ibid.*

43. *Ibid.*
44. *Ibid.*
45. *Ibid.*
46. Fiji, once praised as a showcase of democracy and harmonious racial relations, turned into a place of fear and ethnic and religious intolerance following the military coup and seizure of power by Brig. Gen. Sitiveni Rabuka in 1987. Apparently no real solution to the political problems is in sight since various grovernments' officials, including those of the United States and Australia, continue to press for Fiji to institute measures that would be acceptable to all its ethnic groups.
47. Jones, 1937, pp. 172-173.
48. *Ibid.*
49. Yoder, 1977, p. 21.
50. Chambers, 1962, p. 76.
51. *Ibid.*
52. James K. Mathews, 1969, pp. 33-34.
53. Jones, 1937, p. 147.
54. *Ibid.*
55. *Ibid.*
56. *Ibid.*
57. *Ibid.*, p. 149.
58. *Ibid.*, 1940, pp. 166-168.
59. *Ibid.*, 1937, p. 74.
60. *Ibid.*, p. 75.
61. *Ibid.*, p. 182.
62. *The Theology and Missiology of E. Stanley Jones*, p. 7.

Chapter 8

The Way Out of Disunity

To recapitulate, we have seen that the rift between conservative pentecostal-charismatics and the social justice fold stems from the fact that both parties have let the Kingdom get "buried";[1] both have betrayed Christ's spirit and His Divine Revolution, the Kingdom of God, as the vital all-comprehending "principle of unity." The Kingdom has been "smothered" under a "mass of irrelevancies and localisms,"[2] "hidden absolutisms and triumphalisms,"[3] pharisaical preferences, theological biases, and "unconscious unreality."[4]

The misplacement of the only God-given Key to "central unifying authority"[5] and unity of life -- the Kingdom -- by both wings of the Church has resulted in the drawing of a sharp line between the personal and the social, among other compartmentalizations, and the blocking off of the two sides from each other with all the tensing accoutrements of cold war indifferentism, seething suspicion, hostility and caustic criticalness.

The Holy Spirit's Call for Repentance

The Bible is full of compelling affirmation of God's indisputable oneness. The Church does not have to perpetually undercut its evangelical, prophetic witness and effectiveness nor languish in internal antagonisms. The Holy Spirit's call for repentance, renewal, correction, rectification, reformation, reunification and transfromation is there, is clearly, urgently there, otherwise, we would not have written this book.

There is a way to have both sides drawn together in wholeness, integration, a living blend, to be united in view, life, outlook. It is possible, to paraphrase the Apostle Paul, to have these two wings of the Church standing fast and firm in one spirit, with one mind, working side by side, hand in hand for the faith of the Gospel. (See Philippians 1:27). There is a way out of the "cleavage between the social and the personal emphasis," a way to allow the social approach of the faith to belong with the evangelical, for to be "concerned about the one requires concern about the other."[6] There is the certainty that the overarching unity which the Kingdom of God denotes can bring all believers together with respect to "the deeper facts of life -- the unity of experience and the unity of moral and spiritual beliefs and commitments."[7] There is hope for bilateral conversion, repentance, cessation of grieving the Holy Spirit and a formation of a new linkage, a "new bond of unity"[8] perfecting the two folds in "others-regarding, therefore self-dedicating, therefore self-fulfilling and self-releasing"[9] love.

Paying the Price

But there is a hefty price to pay in order intentionally and prayerfully to prepare and to redirect our hearts, minds and beings toward the way to unity. We do not say this glibly. For too long the eye has said to the hand, "Well, I certainly don't need you." (See I Corinthians 12, especially verse 21). Powerful pride and her recalcitrant triplets, stubbornness, rebellion and self-deception, crouch so close, poised to pounce hard on whichever party might utter the first wavering words of *repentance* and remorse. But just as surely as the Lord quickly hears the slightest whisper of the penitent, the Holy Spirit would as quickly and surely pour out His power to "dig the channels from the reservoir of God's boundless resources [mercy, grace, forgiveness, cleansing, ad infinitum] to the tiny pools of our lives" thereby hallowing the moment as our "highest and most sacred and most real."[10]

Close on the heels of repentance which confesses "guilty as charged" must come *conversion*, that "seed moment," that crucial "pivot"[11] on which everything turns and our two wings hear, "Except ye be converted and become as little children ye shall not enter the Kingdom of God," and "Except a man [a church?] be born again he cannot see the Kingdom of God." Can our two wings hear, really hear the Spirit's words within these words? "Conversion and new birth are the deepest needs of this age or any age... .... Every generation needs regeneration -- this one especially."[12]

Can the Church represented in these two distant wings confess and mean this litany of dismal failures? Is the Church ready to say, yes, we're guilty because we have...

1. "lost," "dehydrated," constricted "by the hand of littleness" the Kingdom;[13]

2. offered various conflicts: "fundamentalist-modernist; the social gospel-the individual gospel" -- every issue *except* the Kingdom of God;[14]

3. been asleep regarding impersonal, structural and systemic evil, social and economic injustices, embraced indiscriminately "wolf principles of selfishness, competition and strife,"[15] cozied up to status quo politics and anti-Christian ideology, not challenged "the whole concept of force which militarism holds,"[16] obligated ourselves morally and psychologically by tailoring our moral standards to the needs of the people who are running the world;[17] [Conservative Pentecostal-Charismatics, please stand.]

4. equated the proclamation of the Gospel and fulfillment of its demands solely with seeking to eradicate slums and poverty, denied the Person and power of the Holy Spirit, shunned and feared and despised His gifts, refused the revelation and call to spiritual warfare against unseen forces; [Liberal Social-Justice Leg, please stand.]

5. failed to cooperate with each other as the family of God and in line with the Kingdom which is the cooperative order, but rather have expressed ourselves as in a competitive "ecclesiastical race"[18] and acted as if our brand of belief, our particular church were an end in itself, as if we were the only unclogged channel of God's grace;[19]

6. equated the Kingdom of God with the Church and been preoccupied with relativisms and not the center of life;

7. compartmentalized, engaged in flagrant unbelief -- "keeping Christ out of any area of life and acting as though He were not the Son of Man"[20] -- and have not fully and genuinely lived out what we claim to be but have rather been lacking in a clear dedication to our major cause, the Kingdom;[21]

8. gone down every dead-end road of self-seeking and self-allegiance, conducted our lives on every ground except that of repentance, freedom for others and extending the hand of forgiveness and reconciliation

to those of a different stripe?

The list could go on. But a cataloguing of wrongs will at best evoke no more than a perfunctory concurring nod of one or two heads.

Launching the Torpedo

We've made the point that Christians of both wings are only partially revolutionized vis-a-vis the Kingdom of God. To call attention to a check-list of sins is not done to enlarge the controversy nor to elicit a flimsy, half-hearted admission of always falling short of the Kingdom of God. Although it has been tacitly acknowledged that the Kingdom is both radical and conservative by its very nature and cannot, therefore, be strictly identified with one extreme or the other, perhaps it needs to be stated explicitly that the Kingdom of God as Jesus interpreted and illustrated it is "radically conserative and conservatively radical, is never outgrown or outmoded, or outdated -- it is historical, contemporaneous, and futuristic. It is all three in one."[22] It is "the same yet unfolding." The more you see the more there is to see. "It is static and dynamic, fixed and unfolding."[23] To repeat, this recitation of failures is not presented to send either side scurrying into an immobilizing niche of self-justification. It is an attempt to cause each party to face honestly differences and sins in the hope that conservative and liberal alike will be driven to their knees at the feet of Jesus.

Stanley Jones warned that to put primary emphasis on the Kingdom is to "launch a torpedo and incur resentment and resistance."[24] We might wish there were such a thing as a mythical, friendly, surgical torpedo which we could launch that would not blow both groups out of the waters of complacency and deceptive quiet before the storm, but would just tickle them up a bit and nudge them closer together. Even deadly accurate Tomahawk missles are, for whatever unforeseen reason, known to go astray and do collateral damage mostly to innocent civilians. But such fantasizing belongs in a Monty Python movie. Even so, we have decided to ram full steam ahead, take aim, and fire the torpedo of the Kingdom at both sides. Before this dubious metaphor breaks down, we hasten to add that a launched torpedo wonderfully concentrates the minds of those in its path. Similarly, it is our sole aim and prayer that the Kingdom, now launched (re-launched?) at the conservative pentecostal-charismatic and liberal social justice wings, will galvanize their attention and cause the two groups 1) *to surrender themselves to and come under the discipline of the Kingdom of God* -- the Unshakable Kingdom, the Absolute Order; the Unchangeable Person, the Absolute Person -- making the Kingdom the center of the Church's message and endeavor[25] and 2) *to surrender to each other* in covenant relationship to keep the Kingdom first. The Church must begin to act as one -- fundamentally and basically.[26] Nothing else must matter except the Kingdom. We welcome the reverberating echo of earlier words: ***when the Church***, i.e., the two wings, determines ...

1) to no longer be an end in itself,
2) that everything it does is relative to and merely approximates this Kingdom,
3) that it succeeds only as it becomes "a cameo of the new order and has interests and attitudes as wide as the Kingdom,"[27] and
4) to "lose itself and find itself in something higher than itself,"[28]

only then will unity come.

Self-Renunciation Is the Kingdom Key

Only this Kingdom key-note of *self-renunciation* will save the two wings from self-righteousness and a holier-than-thou attitude, which, it may be emphasized is an ever-present snare.[29] The Kingdom "strikes a dart straight at the heart of self-sufficiency..."[30] All the old clashes will not only remain but be intensified until and unless the unsurrendered self which is the pentecostal-charismatic wing and the unsurrendered self which is the social justice wing are completely surrendered to "something beyond [themselves], the Kingdom."[31] Once surrendered to the central loyalty which is the Kingdom, the two wings are free and enabled to surrender to each other, to love one another because they each are loyal to and love Something (the Kingdom) and Someone (Christ) higher than themselves.[32]

Such surrender to the dynamic working of the Kingdom not only heightens and opens up the one side to the other, fosters the spirit of cooperation, creates redemptive action, love of truth, and wholeness, is incentive for oneness, fulfills each and adds something lacking in each,[33] cross-fertilizes each other mentally and spiritually,[34] but also fashions and positions the new living blended party or "new man" out of the two for fellowship and meaningful service, witness and moral authority in a fractured world. After all, the charismatic together with the social-justice gospel are alternate beats of Jesus' heart.[35]

Isn't it absurd that Christianity is still trying to fly with one wing? This startling observation by Stanley Jones cannot be equaled for crisp articulation and laser-beam accuracy:

> The Christian faith has often been trying to fly with one wing -- the living Christ as expression of the living order, the Kingdom as a task and hope. We are now seeing more clearly that to fly with one wing is to go round in circles, be that one wing the Person or the Order. It must be both -- the Person and the Order. Each is unique, but coming together they make a uniqueness unparalleled.[36]

Are we ready to "see more clearly" how ludicrous it is for our two wings to keep on trying to fly independently, the one from the other? The one wing flapping one way and the other wing flapping the opposite way serves only to keep the Church in a crippling, self-circling holding pattern, while the world looks on askance, perhaps perplexed, but mostly amused and cynical.

This pathetic picture makes the need for the two wings to come together and to work together in and for the Kingdom emphatic and urgent. No one branch of the Church can attempt the task alone. The task -- the conversion of the whole of life -- is greater than any one group can handle.[37] Stanley Jones tells it like it is: "People must not only hear about the Kingdom of God, but must see it in actual operation, on a small scale perhaps, and in imperfect form, but a real demonstration nevertheless. Little islands of cooperation amid the raging seas of competition are what is needed."[38]

What better place for this "demonstration" to come to life than in the Church reunited? Is it too much to hope and pray and work for an end to anemic approximations of the Kingdom, which is all the two wings, left to their own devices, desires and strengths can muster? Apart from the miracle-working power of the Holy Spirit, the task of coming together around the Kingdom, the task of converting the whole of life -- inside and outside the Church -- would be unthinkable and beyond reach. But I am reminded of the edifying prophecy given to Sharon Daugherty in anointed song at the 1989 "Word Explosion" at Victory Christian Center: "Jesus, [we] will obey you now. [We] will move in your power. You will take [us] from strength to strength. Your grace is sufficient for [us]."

The Kingdom of God. Is it secret? If it is secret, it is an open secret.

And the secret simply is this:

1) To repent. To change the mind. To turn around and go in the opposite direction.

2) To be converted, initially and in the life-long process. To live facing Jesus, to belong to Him.

3) To surrender -- the individual, social, economic, national self -- once-for-all, day-by-day, to that which is Higher, Christ and His Kingdom.

Why surrender? For this stupendous reason: "Now the Divine Self-surrender to us has been complete. The cross is its sign. God can go no further; he has gone to the utmost limit. The one thing lacking is our self-surrender. When that comes love breaks into being. It is spontaneous, inevitable."[39]

Is the Kingdom the key to unity? The Way, the only Way, to unity of expression and experience, of ethical and spiritual commitment? We believe it is. Listen, believe, receive, abide in and give yourself to the truth of this simple faith statement: "Around Jesus and His message, the Kingdom, we do not seek to find unity, we have it. All we need is to express it."[40] The emphasis of the Kingdom of God is, as Stanley Jones says, "...carthartic to our thinking, cleansing away minor issues and bringing us to grips with the really great ones. That is important, for it is the minor things that divide us and it is the central things in which we are really one. The Kingdom would unite us."[41]

The Kingdom alone would unite us. Apart from becoming Kingdom-conscious there is no hope for unity.[42] Surrendered, receptive, obedient to the Kingdom, all things are possible. We pray boldly, with heart's peace that we are heard of our Heavenly Father and do receive His answer: 'Come, Holy Spirt, cleanse us, forgive us. Brood over two willful wings. Apply the precious blood of Jesus to the broken places, as indeed You already have. Help us to surrender self-centered self, to receive and to obey Christ and His Kingdom *now*! Amen!'

Notes

1. Jones, 1937, p. 15.
2. *Ibid.*

3. Rodgers, 1990, p. 804.
4. Chambers, p. 76.
5. Jones, 1937, p. 13.
6. Mathews and Mathews, p. 9.
7. *Ibid.* , p. 10.
8. *Ibid.*
9. Jonees, 1972, p. 154.
10. Mathews and Mathews, p. 132.
11. *Ibid.*, p. 119.
12. *Ibid.*, p. 120.
13. Jones, 1972, pp. 18, 21, 30.
14. *Ibid.*
15. *Ibid.*, 1931, p. 15.
16. *Ibid.*, p. 20.
17. *Ibid.*, 1939, pp. 116-117.
18. *Ibid.*, 1937, p. 20.
19. *Ibid.*, 1939, p. 152.
20. *Ibid.*, p. 96.
21. *Ibid.*, p. 108.
22. *Ibid.*, 1972, p. 170.
23. *Ibid.*
24. *Ibid.*, 1939, p. 179.
25. *Ibid.*, 1972, p. 65.
26. *Ibid.*, 1939, p. 152.
27. *Ibid.*, 1972, p. 81.
28. *Ibid.*
29. *Ibid.*, 1939, p. 188.
30. *Ibid.*, 1972, p. 154.
31. *Ibid.*, p. 93.
32. *Ibid.*, p. 94.
33. *Ibid.*, 1939, p. 184.
34. *Ibid.*, p. 189.
35. *Ibid.*, p. 190.
36. *Ibid.*, 1972, pp. 295-296.
37. *Ibid.*, 1937, pp. 182-183.
38. *Ibid.*, 1939, p. 192.
39. Mathews and Mathews, p. 122.
40. *Ibid.*, p. 10.
41. Jones, 1937, p. 183.
42. *Ibid.*

Glossary

Liberalism

American Protestant liberalism appeared in the late nineteenth and early twentieth centuries. It believed in a world which could be known and controlled by man, a world which was moving in the direction of material progress and was "gradually bringing mankind to a more or less perfected state of personal and social existence on earth."[1] This liberal faith included both "a commitment to justice and opportunity for the disadvantaged" as well as a belief in the ability of government to provide this justice and opportunity.[2]

George M. Marsden, a leading historian of American religion, approaches liberal American Protestantism in the late nineteenth and early twentieth centuries from a different perspective. Liberalism, he writes, "was a movement designed to save Protestantism" from Darwinism, biblical criticism, the social sciences and the widespread secularization of American society.[3] In order to defend its religious principles, liberal Protestantism "held that the basis of religion is the sense of absolute dependence." [All good religion majors will recognize the silent allusion to the German theologian and philosopher, Friedrich Ernst Daniel Schleiermacher (1772-1829), who is credited with fathering the view that religion is the feeling of absolute dependence upon God.] This sense of absolute dependence was a feeling or an emotion, not dependent on reason or science.[4] In this way liberalism preserved a sanctuary for Christian truth, secure from the assaults of science and secular society.

In either case, whether we approach Protestant liberalism as an accomodation to or as a retreat from the scientific and technological revolutions of the eighteenth and nineteenth centuries, these revolutions were the decisive events in the origin and development of what we describe as the advocates of liberal social justice in the contemporary Christian church in America.

The Social Gospel

The social gospel was an integral part of American Protestant liberalism. For those who believed and worked for the prophetic vision of the social gospel, the Kingdom of God was "a possibility within history." The exponents of the social gospel "were so confident of human goodness as to be sure that men could be educated to choose the good and to contribute directly to 'the building of the kingdom.'"[5]

Another description of American Protestant liberalism focuses on its theology and on its successful effort "to adjust the ancient faith" of Christianity "to the modern world."[6] In an age of scientific discovery and technological progress all areas of human concern, including religion, are subject to intense critical analysis. Shailer Mathews, one of the leaders of the so-called "Chicago School" of liberal Protestantism, declared in 1928 that "Jesus and his words must be understood in accordance with historical relativity."[7]

If the Bible can be correctly interpreted like any other historical or liberary document, then Christianity loses its claim to unique divine authority. Liberal theology therefore assumes that all cultures experience something which they call "religion" but that different cultures express this universal experience in different ways.[8] No one religion is any more valid than another religion. All claims to religious truth are relative.

Post-Liberalism

Post-liberalism retreats from complete religious relativism by attempting to establish what is "distinctive" and "authentic" about the Christian faith. Post-liberalism defends Christianity "in its purity against all other competing faiths both ancient and modern."[9] For post-liberalism the truth of Christianity lies not in its universality but in the lives of Christians who have been changed by it. The task of post-liberal theology is to articulate "the convictions of those who have been personally and socially transformed by a religious community."[10]

The liberal social justice stream of American Christianity is part of this heritage of liberalism and post-liberalism. However, when we use the term "liberal social justice," we refer to Christians who share a prophetic witness against any kind of systemic or institutional injustice, regardless of whether the injustice occurs in economic, social or political institutions. We do not focus on any particular issue. Rather, we believe God is concerned about all types of institutional injustice, just as He is concerned about all types of personal or individual injustice. Society can be a "good tree" and help individuals or the social order can be a "bad tree" and thus hurt individuals. (See Matthew 7:17-20NIV).

Evangelicalism

In contrast to both liberalism and post-liberalism, evangelical Christianity insists that the Bible is the revelatory record of God's objective and unique truth about Himself and about His relationship to man. This truth is "not conditioned by the personal experience of the individual" or by the application of modern scientific methods of historical criticism.[11] Richard Quebedeaux, one of the foremost popular writers on the evangelical movement, states that in addition to accepting the absolute authority of the Bible, evangelicals have been personally converted to Christ through the experience of being born again and are committed to share this good news of God's redemptive grace with others.[12]

James Davison Hunter, a sociologist specializing in the study of American Evangelicalism, emphasizes the theological and sociological diversity of contemporary American Evangelicals. However, he defines the "doctrinal core" of contemporary Evengelicalism as belief in "the Bible" as "the inerrant Word of God ... belief in the divinity of Christ, and ... belief in the efficacy of Christ's life, death, and physical resurrection for the salvation of the human soul."[13]

Evangelicalism, according to Marsden, was "a style as well as a set of Protestant beliefs about the Bible and Christ's saving work."[14] Moreover, during the 1950s and 1960s Marsden says that the "simplest definition of an evangelical ... was 'anyone who likes Billy Graham.'"[15] In more complex theological terms, however, Marsden agrees with Hunter that "[t]he essential evangelical beliefs include (1) the Reformation doctrine of the final authority of the Bible, (2) the real historical character of God's saving work recorded in Scripture, (3) salvation to eternal life based on the redemptive work of Christ, (4) the importance of evangelism and missions, and (5) the importance of a spiritually transformed life."[16]

Pentecostalism

American pentecostalism is one branch of the evangelical movement. Its beginning is usually traced to a revival held at the Azusa Street Mission in Los Angeles in 1906.[17] Like evangelicals, pentecostals believe in the primacy and divine authority of The Scriptures. Pentecostals and evangelicals also agree on the importance of both the new birth in Christ and of evangelism or sharing the good news with others. However, pentecostals are distinctive in their emphasis on "the person and work of the Holy Spirit."[18] One commentator has stated that the "central doctrine of pentecostalism ... is 'the abiding possibility and importance of the supernatural element ... particularly as contained in the manifestation of the Spirit.'"[19] Pentecostals believe that all the gifts of the Spirit listed by Paul in I Corinthians 12:8-10 -- wisdom, knowledge, faith, healing, miracles, prophecy, discernment, speaking in tongues and interpretation of tongues -- are available to Christians today.

In a forum conducted at the Asia Pacific Theological Seminary and published in *Paraclete*, a journal published by the Assemblies of God, the largest pentecostal denomination, Dave Oleson said, "To me, this is what it means to be Pentecostal: to be responsive to the moving of the Holy Spirit, that experiential aspect of it, allowing the Spirit to work in the supernatural."[20] Another participant in the forum, Robert Menzies, emphasized baptism in the Holy Spirit as the distinctive pentecostal experience. Menzies says that "the key is that we [pentecostals] see it as something different, logically distinct, from conversion."[21]

The best recent effort to explore the nineteenth century origins of American Pentecostalism and to explain its connections with Evangelicalism and Fundamentalism is Donald W. Dayton's *Theological Roots of Pentecostalism*. In identifying a theology for the Pentecostal Movement, Dayton relies on Aimee Semple McPherson, founder of the International Church of the Foursquare Gospel, who used four concepts from the New Testament to summarize her "basic message." There four concepts were salvation, baptism of the Holy Spirit, physical healing and the second coming of Jesus Christ.[22]

Neo-Pentecostalism

The American pentecostal movement of the early twentieth century produced scores of new churches and denominations. However, the influence of the pentecostal movement was not confined to these new religious bodies. Eventually, the mainline Protestant and Catholic churches were also affected by pentecostalism. Members of these traditional churches who accept the pentecostal experience are called neo-pentecostals.[23]

The Charismatic Renewal Movement

Finally, the term "charismatic renewal" refers to a revival which began in small pentecostal churches after World War II and which by the late 1950s and early 1960s had spread to mainline Protestant and Catholic churches.[24] The charismatic renewal grew out of the spiritual emptiness of contemporary American culture and out of dissatisfaction with the response of the traditional churches to that emptiness. A Protestant campus minister who describes himself as a "closet charismatic" believes the charismatic movement is "a valid judgment on the church's accommodation to and endorsement of a culture which has become increasingly debasing to the human spirit."[25]

In this study we mean by charismatic any Christian who accepts the empowering presence and redemptive gifts of the Holy Spirit.

Notes

1. Cauthen, 1971, p. xvii.
2. Fox, p. 6.
3. Marsden, p. 32.
4. *Ibid.*, p. 35.
5. Handy, p. 10.
6. Cauthen, 1962, p. 5.
7. Mathews, 1971, p. 12.
8. Willimon, p. 82.
9. Cauthen, 1962, p. 229.
10. Willimon, p. 82.
11. Ellingsen, p. 50.
12. Quebedeaux, 1978, pp. 6-7.
13. Hunter, 1983, p. 7.
14. Marsden, p. 2.

15. *Ibid.*, p. 6.
16. *Ibid.*, pp. 4-5.
17. Harrell, p. 11.
18. Zimmerman, p. 36.
19. Gee, p. 3.
20. Menzies, p. 4.
21. *Ibid.*, p. 5.
22. Dayton, 1991, p. 21.
23. Harrell, p. ix.
24. *Ibid.*, p. 5.
25. Snyder, p. 880.

For Further Reading and Reflection

Another interpretation of the social gospel, which is different from Robert Handy's interpretation, quoted in this glossary, that the Kingdom of God could in fact be established on earth through the religious zeal of men of good will, is contained in Donald K. Gorrell's *The Age of Social Responsibility: The Social Gospel in the Progressive Era, 1900-1920* published by Mercer University Press (Macon, Georgia) in 1988. Gorrell interprets the social gospel as being more of a secular than a religious movement in the late nineteenth and early twentieth centuries in the United States. Gorrell writes that the social gospel was based more on the secular concept of "social responsibility" than on the specifically religious idea of the "kingdom of God" or of "Christianizing the social order." P. 7.

For the concept of a pentecostal social gospel see Paul Valliere, *Holy War and Pentecostal Peace*. New York: Seabury, 1983.

> The constructive task of a Pentecostal Social Gospel is to show that an ethic of humility, cultivated conscientiously in the field of social action, can have a formative impact on the progress of justice and peace. P. 135.

William R. Hutchison's *Liberal Protestantism: Realities and Possibilities*, published by Pilgrim Press in 1986, is another source on contemporary liberalism in American Protestant Christianity. Hutchison's book is excerpted in a two-part series in *The Christian Century*, Past Imperfect: History and the Prospect for Liberalism -- I, vol. 103 (January 1-8, 1986) pp. 11-15; and Past Imperfect: History and the Prospect for Liberalism -- II, vol. 103 (January 15, 1986) pp. 42-46. *The Christian Century* is the leading popular magazine of the liberal Protestant establishment.

Hutchison also edited an earlier collection entitled *American Protestant Thought: The Liberal Era* published by Harper & Row in 1968.

A recent book by Robert Booth Fowler, *Unconventional Partners: Religion and Liberal Culture in the United States*, argues that mainline Protestant and Catholic churches are not politically effective because their members do not support the controversial liberal positions proclaimed by church leaders. According to Fowler these church leaders fail to appreciate the fact that the rank and file participate in church activities because religion provides an alternative to and a refuge from political and social problems. See Martin E. Marty's review of Fowler's book, Filling in the Gaps of Liberal Culture, *The Christian Century*, vol. 106 (November 8, 1989) pp. 1019-1022.

For an analysis of the contemporary conflict between liberals and evangelicals from a social science perspective see Robert Wuthnow, *The Struggle for America's Soul: Evangelicals, Liberals and Secularism.* Grand Rapids, Michigan: Eerdmans, 1989. An earlier book by Wuthnow, *The Restructuring of American Religion: Society and Faith Since World War II*, is excerpted in Divided We Fall: America's Two Civil Religions, *The Christian Century*, vol. 104 (April 20, 1988) pp. 395-399.

The leading Catholic magazine on political, social and economic issues is *America*. An insightful article supporting the thesis of our book is DiIanni, Faith and Justice: A Delicate Balance, vol. 161 (July 15-22, 1989) pp. 32-34, which states that the liberal social justice advocates must have strong Christian roots to be truly effective.

Bibliography

Amstutz, John. 1985. Beyond Pentecost: A Study of Some Sociological Dimensions of New Testament Church Growth From the Book of Acts. *Essays on Apostolic Themes: Studies in Honor of Howard M. Ervin*, ed. Paul Elbert. Peabody, Massachusetts: Hendrickson, pp. 208-225.

Bartleman, Frank. 1982. *Another Wave of Revival*, ed. John G. Myers. Springdale, Pennsylvania: Whitaker House.

Beaman, Jay. 1982. *Pentecostal Pacifism: The Origin, Development and Rejection of Pacific Belief Among Pentecostals.* M. Div. Thesis. North American Baptist Seminary. Sioux Falls, South Dakota.

Bittlinger, Arnold. 198 The Significance of Charismatic Experiences for the Mission of the Church. *International Review of Mission.* Vol. 75 (April) pp. 117-122.

Breckenridge, James F. 1986. Repentance. *Decision.* Vol. 27 (July-August) pp. 31-33.

Brown, Dale W. 1978. *Understanding Pietism.* Grand Rapids, Michigan: Eerdmans.

Bruce, Carla. 1986. Do Not Speculate. *The Upper Room Daily Devotional Guide*. (May-June) p. 60. Nashville, Tennessee: The Upper Room.

Cauthen, Kenneth. 1962. *The Impact of American Religious Liberalism.* New York: Harper & Row.

_____. 1971. Introduction: The Life and Thought of Shailer Mathews. Shailer Mathews, *Jesus on Social Institutions*, pp. xiii-lxxiii.

Chambers, Oswald. 1963. *My Utmost For His Highest.* Westwood, New Jersey: Barbour.

Chappell, Paul G. 1991. Interview with Authors at School of Theology and Missions, Oral Roberts University. Tulsa, Oklahoma. (March 11).

Davis, Rex. 1978. *Locusts and Wild Honey: The Charismatic Renewal and the Ecumenical Movement.* Geneva, Switzerland: World Council of Churches.

Dayton, Donald W. 1976. *Discovering an Evangelical Heritage.* New York: Harper & Row.

_____. 1991. *Theological Roots of Pentecostalism.* Peabody, Massachusetts: Hendrickson.

Deanhardt, Michael C. 1987. Writer Challenges Conservatives (Letter to Editor). *The South Carolina United Methodist Advocate.* (January 1).

Dempster, Murray W. 1987. Pentecostal Social Concern and the Biblical Mandate of Social Justice. *Pneuma: The Journal of the Society for Pentecostal Studies.* Vol. 9 (Fall) pp. 129-153.

_____. 1989. Review of Jay Beaman, *Pentecostal Pacifism. Pneuma.* Vol. 11 (Fall) pp. 59-64.

Dods, Marcus. No Date. *The First Epistle to the Corinthians. The Expositor's Bible*, ed. W. Robertson Nicoll. Cincinnati: Jennings and Graham.

Duin, Julia. 1988. Mainline Methodist Denounce Liberal Trends. *Christianity Today.* Vol 32 (February 5) pp. 51-52.

Dunn, James D. G. 1984. Models of Christian Community in the New Testament. *Strange Gifts? A Guide to Charismatic Renewal*, ed. David Martin and Peter Mullen. Oxford, England: Basil Blackwell.

Ellingsen, Mark. 1984. The Difference Between Liberals and Evangelicals. *Christianity Today.* Vol. 28 (February 17) p. 50.

Fowler, Robert Booth. 1982. *A New Engagement: Evangelical Political Thought, 1966-1976.* Grand Rapids, Michigan: Eerdmans.

Fox, Richard. 1987. The Liberal Ethic and the Spirit of Protestantism. *The Center Magazine.* Vol. 20 (September-October) pp. 4-14.

Gallup, George, Jr. and Jim Castelli. 1989. *The People's Religion: American Faith in the 90s.* New York: Macmillan.

Gee, Donald. 1967. *Wind and Flame.* Croyden, Surrey, England: Heath Press.

Georgianna, Sharon Linzey. 1988. The American Assemblies of God: Spiritual Emphasis and Social Activism. *Faces of Renewal: Studies in Honor of Stanley M. Horton Presented on His 70th Birthday*. Peabody, Massachusetts: Hendrickson.

Gerlach, Luther P. and Virginia H. Hine. 1970. *People, Power, Change: Movements of Social Transformation*. Indianapolis: Bobbs-Merrill.

Graham, Gordon. 1986. Justice, Charity and the Third World. *Modern Theology*. Vol. 3 (October) pp. 21-33.

Handy, Robert T. (ed.). 1966. *The Social Gospel in America, 1870-1920: Gladden, Ely and Rauschenbusch. A Library of Protestant Thought*. New York: Oxford University Press.

Harden, Ruth W. 1985. Cues. *The Upper Room Daily Devotional Guide*. (September-October, 1985) p. 11. Nashville, Tennessee: The Upper Room.

Harrell, David E., Jr. 1975. *All Things Are Possible: The Healing and Charismatic Revivals in Modern America*. Bloomington, Indiana: Indiana University Press.

Henry, Carl F. H. 1989. The New Coalitions. *Christianity Today*. Vol. 33 (November 17) pp. 26-28.

Hollenweger, Walter J. 1986. After Twenty Years Research on Pentecostalism. *International Review of Mission*. Vol. 75 (January) pp. 3-12.

Hunter, James Davison. 1983. *American Evangelicalism: Conservative Religion and the Quandry of Modernity*. New Brunswick, New Jersey: Rutgers University Press.

_____. 1987. *Evangelicalism: The Coming Generation*. Chicago, Illinois: University of Chicago Press.

Hutchison, William R. 1985. Does Liberal Protestantism Have an American Future? *The Center Magazine*. Vol. 18 (November-December) pp. 9-16.

Jones, E. Stanley. 1925. *The Christ of the Indian Road*. New York: Grosset & Dunlap.

_____. 1931. *The Christ of the Mount: A Working Philosophy of Life*. New York and Nashville: Abingdon-Cokesbury.

_____. 1936. *Victorious Living*. New York: Abingdon.

_____. 1937. *The Choice Before Us*. New York: Abingdon.

_____. 1939. *Along the Indian Road*. New York: Abindon.

_____. 1940. *Is the Kingdom of God Realism?* New York and Nashville: Abingdon-Cokesbury.

_____. 1944. *The Christ of the American Road.* New York and Nashville: Abingdon-Cokesbury.

_____. 1946. *The Way.* New York: Abingdon-Cokesbury.

_____. 1948. *Mahatma Gandhi: An Interpretation.* New York: Abingdon-Cokesbury.

_____. 1949. *The Way to Power and Poise.* New York: Abingdon-Cokesbury.

_____. 1951. *How to Be a Transformed Person.* New York: Abingdon-Cokesbury.

_____. 1968. *A Song of Ascents: A Spiritual Autobiography.* Nashville and New York: Abingdon.

_____. 1970. *The Reconstruction of the Church: On What Pattern?* Nashville: Abingdon.

_____. 1972. *The Unshakeable Kingdom and the Unchangeable Person.* Nashville: Abingdon.

_____. 1983. *Gandhi: Portrayal of a Friend.* Nashville: Abingdon. Reprint of *Mahatma Gandhi: An Interpretation.*

Kantzer, Kenneth S. 1980. The Charismatics Among Us. *Christianity Today.* Vol. 24 (February 22) pp. 25-29.

Kelley, John. 1988. Time for the Grace of Doing Nothing. *The Christian Century.* Vol. 105 (October 26) pp. 940-941.

Kirill, Archbishop. 1988. Renewal of Humanity, Unity of the Church and the New Thinking. *The Ecumenical Review.* Vol. 40 (April) pp. 256-266.

Koenig, A. and Henry I. Lederle. 1990. *Systematic Theology: Study Guide 2 for THB 301-X (Ecumenical Theology).* Pretoria, South Africa: University of South Africa, rev. ed.

Lederle, Henry I. 1986. The Charismatic Movement -- The Ambiguous Challenge. *Missionalia: Journal of South African Missiological Society.* Vol. 14 (August) pp. 61-75.

Levine, Daniel H. 1987. Holiness, Faith, Power, Politics. (Review Essay). *Journal for the Scientific Study of Religion.* Vol. 26, pp. 551-561.

Liardon, Roberts. 1989. *Run to the Battle.* Tulsa, Oklahoma: Harrison House.

Lovelace, Richard F. 1979. *Dynamics of Spiritual Life: An Evangelical Theology of Renewal.* Downers Grove, Illinois: InterVarsity.

Marsden, George M. 1991. *Understanding Fundamentalism and Evangelicalism.* Grand Rapids, Michigan: Eerdmans.

Mathews, Eunice Jones and James K. Mathews (compilers). 1972. *Selections from E. Stanley Jones: Christ and Human Need.* Nashville and New York: Abingdon.

Mathews, James K. 1969. *A Church Truly Catholic.* Nashville and New York: Abingdon.

Mathews, Shailer. 1971. *Jesus on Social Institutions. Lives of Jesus Series*, ed. Leander E. Keck. Philadelphia, Pennsylvania: Fortress.

Moberg, David O. 1972. *The Great Reversal: Evangelism Versus Social Concern. Evangelical Perspectives,* ed. John Warwick Montogomery. Philadelphia, Pennsylvania: J. B. Lippincott.

Menzies, Robert P. (ed.). 1992. The Essence of Pentecostalism. *Paraclete: A Journal Concerning the Person and Work of the Holy Spirit*, Vol. 26 (Summer) pp. 1-9.

Mouw, Richard J. 1990. Humility, Hope and the Divine Slowness. *The Christian Century.* Vol. 107 (April 11) pp. 364-368.

Muck, Terry. 1988. Holy Indignation. *Christianity Today.* Vol 32. (October 21) pp. 14-15.

Neuhaus, Richard John. 1990. Religion and Public Life: The Continuing Conversation. *The Christian Century*. Vol. 107 (July 11-18) pp. 669-673.

Patijn, C. L. 1988. "The Responsible Society" in Retrospect. *The Ecumenical Review.* Vol. 40 (July-October) pp. 367-371.

Petrella, Lidia Susana Vaccaro de. 1986. The Tension Between Evangelism and Social Action in the Pentecostal Movement. *International Review of Mission.* Vol. 75 (January) pp. 34-38.

Phillips, J. B. 1956. *New Testament Christianity.* New York: Macmillan.

Pinnock, Clark. 1981. Opening the Church to the Charismatic Dimension. *Christianity Today.* Vol. 25 (June 12) p. 16.

Poloma, Margaret M. 1982. *The Charismatic Movement: Is There a New Pentecost? Social Movement Past and Present*, ed. Irwin Sanders. Boston, Massachusetts: Twayne.

_____. 1988. The Charismatic Movement and Loving Communities: An Analysis of Growth. *Faces of Renewal.* (See Georgianna, S. L. for full citation).

Quebedeaux, Richard. 1978. *The Wordly Evangelicals.* New York: Harper & Row.

_____. 1983. *The New Charismatics II.* San Francisco: Harper & Row.

Rifkin, Jeremy with Ted Howard. 1979. *The Emerging Order: God in the Age of Scarcity*. New York: G. P. Putnam's Sons.

Robeck, Cecil M., Jr. 1987. Pentecostals and Social Ethics. *Pneuma*. Vol. 9 (Fall) pp. 103-107.

Robison, James. 1987. What Have We Learned in the Midst of the Shaking? *Restoration*. (November-December) pp. 3-9.

Rogers, Cornish R. On Being "Global" and "Contextual." *The Christian Century*. Vol. 107 (September 5-12) p. 804.

Roelofs, H. Mark. 1988. Liberation Theology: The Recovery of Biblical Radicalism. *American Political Science Review*. Vol. 82 (June) pp. 549-566.

Ryn, Claes. 1984. The Things of Caesar: Toward the Delimitation of Politics. *Essays on Christianity and Political Philosophy*, ed. George W. Carey and James V. Schall. Lanham, Maryland: University Press of America.

Sahlberg, Carl Erick. 1985. *The Pentecostal Movement: Five Case Studies*. Nairobi, Kenya: Evangel Publishing House.

Smith, Timothy L. 1957. *Revivalism and Social Reform in Mid-Nineteenth Century America*. New York and Nashville: Abingdon.

Snyder, Dean J. 1983. Confessions of a Closet Charismatic. *The Christian Century*. Vol. 100 (October 5) pp. 878-881.

Soeldner, Thomas. 1989. Charismatic Churches and the Struggle Against Apartheid: A Dispute. *The Christian Century*. Vol. 106 (January 4-11) pp. 16; 18-19.

Stafford, Tim. 1989. Fruit of the Vineyard. *Christianity Today*. Vol. 33 (November 17) pp. 35-36.

Stockwell, Eugene L. 1986. Editorial. *International Review of Mission*. Vol. 75 (April) pp. 113-116.

Stott, John R. W. 1981. Setting the Spirit Free.*Christianity Today*. Vol. 25 (June 12) pp. 17-21.

Suenens, Cardinal Leon Joseph and Dom Helder Camara. 1979. *Charismatic Renewal and Social Action: A Dialogue. Malines Document 3*. Ann Arbor, Michigan: Servant Books, pp. 71-76.

Swierenga, Robert P. 1990. Ethnoreligious Political Behavior in the Mid-Nineteenth Century: Voting, Values, Cultures. *Religion and American Politics: From the Colonial Period to the 1980s*, ed. Mark A. Noll. New York: Oxford University Press.

Synan, Vinson. 1987. Pentecostalism: Varieties and Contribution. *Pneuma*. Vol. 9 (Spring) pp. 31-49.

The Theology and Missiology of E. Stanley Jones: A Compilation from His Books by a Class in the E. Stanley Jones School of World Mission and Evangelism. 1985. Wilmore, Kentucky: Asbury Theological Seminary.

Tileston, Mary Wilder. (ed.). 1928. *Daily Strength for Daily Needs.* New York: Grosset and Dunlap.

Tocqueville, Alexis de. 1969. *Democracy in America*, ed. J. P. Mayer, transl. George Lawrence. Garden City, New York: Doubleday Anchor.

Washington, James M. (ed.). 1991. *A Testament of Hope: The Essential Writings and Speeches of Martin Luther King, Jr.* San Francisco, California: HarperCollins.

Weber, Max. 1947. *The Theory of Social and Economic Organization,* transl. A. M. Henderson and Talcott Parsons. London: the Free Press of Glencoe, Collier-Macmillan.

Willimon, William H. 1987. Answering Pilate: Truth and the Postliberal Church. *The Christian Century.* Vol. 104 (January 28) pp. 82-85.

Yoder, John H. 1972. *The Politics of Jesus.* Grand Rapids, Michigan: Eerdmans.

_____. 1977. *The Original Revolution: Essays on Christian Pacifism.* Scottdale, Pennsylvania: Herald.

Zimmerman, Thomas F. 1981. Priorities and Beliefs of Pentecostals. *Christianity Today.* Vol. 25 (September 4) pp. 36-37.

Index